Modeling Wind Adjustment Factor and Midflame Wind Speed for Rothermel's Surface Fire Spread Model

Patricia L. Andrews

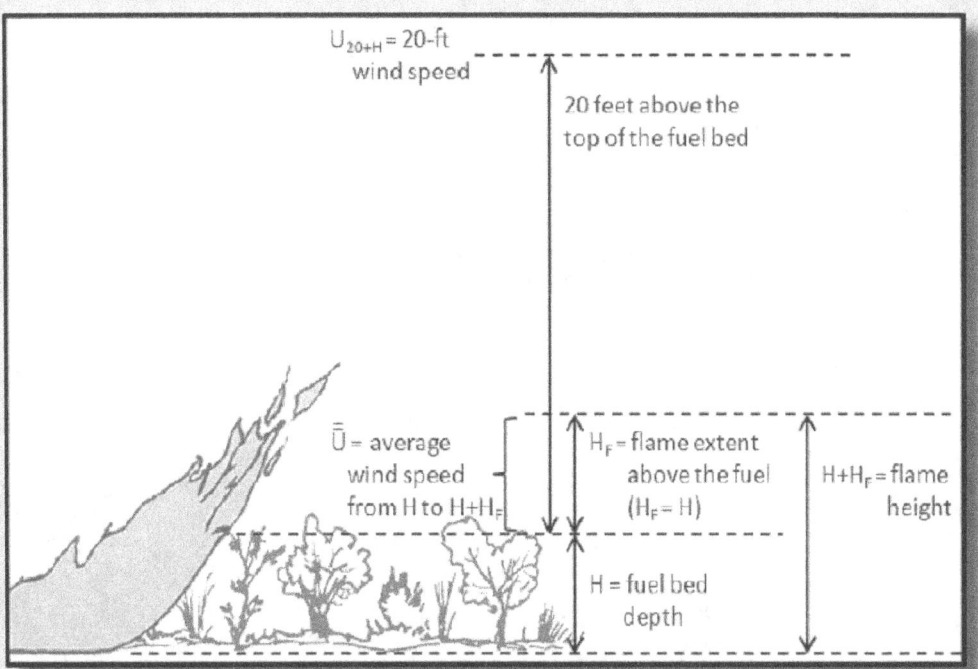

USDA United States Department of Agriculture / Forest Service

Rocky Mountain Research Station

General Technical Report RMRS-GTR-266

January 2012

Andrews, Patricia L. 2012. **Modeling wind adjustment factor and midflame wind speed for Rothermel's surface fire spread model.** Gen. Tech. Rep. RMRS-GTR-266. Fort Collins, CO: U.S. Department of Agriculture, Forest Service, Rocky Mountain Research Station. 39 p.

Abstract

Rothermel's surface fire spread model was developed to use a value for the wind speed that affects surface fire, called midflame wind speed. Models have been developed to adjust 20-ft wind speed to midflame wind speed for sheltered and unsheltered surface fuel. In this report, Wind Adjustment Factor (WAF) model equations are given, and the BehavePlus fire modeling system is used to demonstrate WAF calculation and effect on modeled fire behavior. There are differences in implementation of the same basic wind adjustment models in various fire behavior applications, including the Fireline Handbook and FARSITE. Differences are due to assumptions such as tree shape and rules for transition from sheltered to unsheltered conditions. Specifics are given for differences among WAF tables and calculation applications. This technical documentation is useful to analysts, system developers, fire weather meteorologists, and those who are interested in model background and foundation.

Keywords: wildland fire, fire behavior, fire danger rating, fire modeling, fire spread

Author

Patricia L. Andrews is a Research Physical Scientist with the Fire, Fuel, and Smoke Science Program at the Fire Sciences Laboratory in Missoula, Montana. She has been at the Fire Lab since 1973, serving as Project Leader of the Fire Behavior Research Work Unit from 1992 to 1996. Her research focus is fire behavior prediction and fire danger rating.

Acknowledgments

I thank the following people for helpful review comments: Larry Bradshaw, Jason Forthofer, Chuck McHugh (U.S. Department of Agriculture, Forest Service), and John Saltenberger (U.S. Department of the Interior, Bureau of Land Management). I also thank Faith Ann Heinsch (U.S. Forest Service), who provided valuable technical help and assisted with document preparation.

The BehavePlus fire modeling system computer program is available from http://www.FireModels.org.

You may order additional copies of this publication by sending your mailing information in label form through one of the following media. Please specify the publication title and number.

Publishing Services

Telephone	(970) 498-1392
FAX	(970) 498-1122
E-mail	rschneider@fs.fed.us
Web site	http://www.fs.fed.us/rmrs
Mailing Address	Publications Distribution
	Rocky Mountain Research Station
	240 West Prospect Road
	Fort Collins, CO 80526

Contents

Introduction

Wind is among the most important influences on wildland fire. Fire behavior is strongly affected by wind speed and direction, which vary in time at the scale on the order of hours, minutes, and even seconds. The wind that affects wildland fire is influenced by terrain and vegetation. In addition to horizontal changes across the landscape, wind speed varies vertically with height above the ground. Determining an appropriate wind speed to use in modeling surface fire spread, flame length, and intensity is not a trivial task.

Fire modeling plays an important role in wildland fire and fuel management. For example, the National Fire Danger Rating System (NFDRS) (Deeming and others 1977) indices indicate the level of fire danger for public information and suppression preparedness. The FARSITE fire area simulator (Finney 1998) can be used to model growth of ongoing wildfires for tactical fire suppression decisions. The Fire Program Analysis (FPA) system includes modeling hypothetical fires to evaluate various funding levels (USDA/USDOI 2001; Finney and others 2011). The BehavePlus fire modeling system (Andrews 2011) can be used to develop prescription windows based on desired fire behavior and escaped fire contingency planning.

Rothermel's surface fire spread model (Rothermel 1972) is at the core of most fire behavior, fire danger, fuels management, and fire decision support systems in the United States. The Rothermel model includes the effect of fuel, fuel moisture, slope, and wind speed on surface fire rate of spread and intensity. Wind speed appropriately has a significant effect on modeled fire behavior. The fire model uses "midflame" wind speed, the wind that affects the surface fire.

Wind speed varies with height above the ground. The wind speed at midflame height is generally less than the wind speed above that level. Local winds generated from general winds aloft are slowed by surface friction near the surface, often producing a velocity profile as shown in figure 1.

The U.S. standard for fire weather wind is 20 ft above bare ground, or 20 ft above the vegetation (figure 2). The wind adjustment factor (WAF) adjusts the 20-ft wind speed to a midflame wind. Midflame wind speed is 20-ft wind speed multiplied by WAF. We use the term "wind adjustment factor" rather than "wind reduction factor" to avoid confusion in interpretation. A WAF of 0.40 reduces the 20-ft wind by 60 percent.

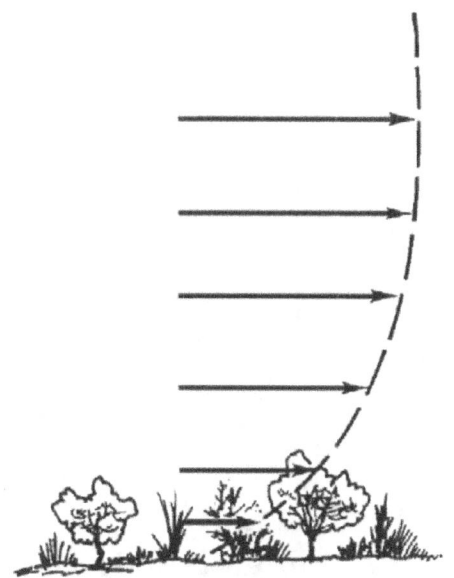

Figure 1—General wind velocity profile near surface (from Rothermel 1983).

USDA Forest Service Gen. Tech. Rep. RMRS-GTR-266. 2012

1

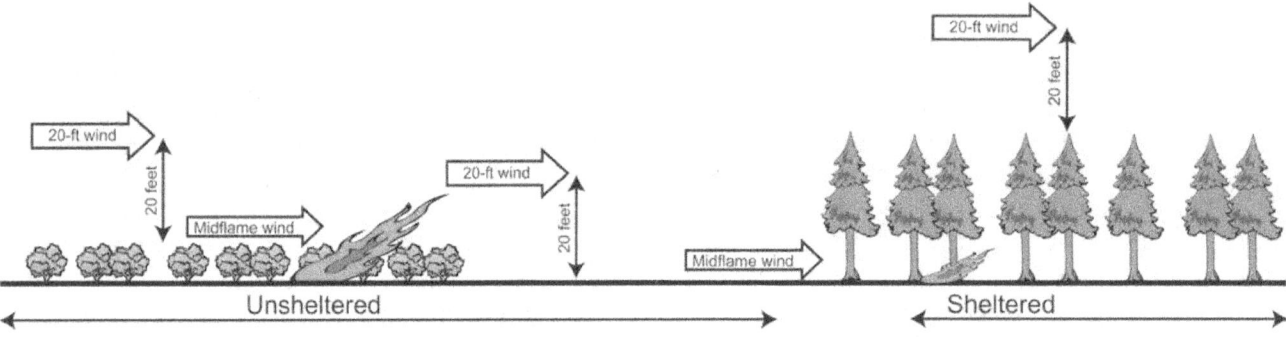

Figure 2—Twenty-ft wind speed is the wind 20 ft above bare ground, surface fuels, or trees. Midflame wind is the wind that affects a surface fire, as required by Rothermel's surface fire spread model.

The various standards for the height of measured and forecasted wind speed should be kept in mind when determining midflame wind (figure 3). Wind measurements are taken at 20 ft above the ground at fire weather stations. Fischer and Hardy (1972) defined the standard for station location as level, cleared areas that are not influenced by surrounding vegetation. At that time, because daily fire weather readings were taken manually, stations were generally located near an office. Remote Automatic Weather Stations (RAWS) now allow location in areas more representative of fire weather, possibly on slopes where it is more difficult to find a site not influenced by surrounding vegetation. For fire weather applications, the U.S. National Weather Service (NWS) usually forecasts 20-ft wind. In some cases, spot weather forecasts are given for midflame (eye level) wind. NWS forecasts and observations for the public are at the 10-m height, the World Meteorological Organization (WMO) standard. The Oklahoma Mesonet includes wind speed at 10 m as a core parameter and wind speed at 2 m as a supplemental parameter (mainly used for agricultural purposes) (McPherson and others 2007). Portable Fire RAWS have masts about 1.8 m (6 ft) above the ground (Bradshaw and others 2003). Handheld measurements are taken in the field using a hand-held anemometer, thus the term "eye level."

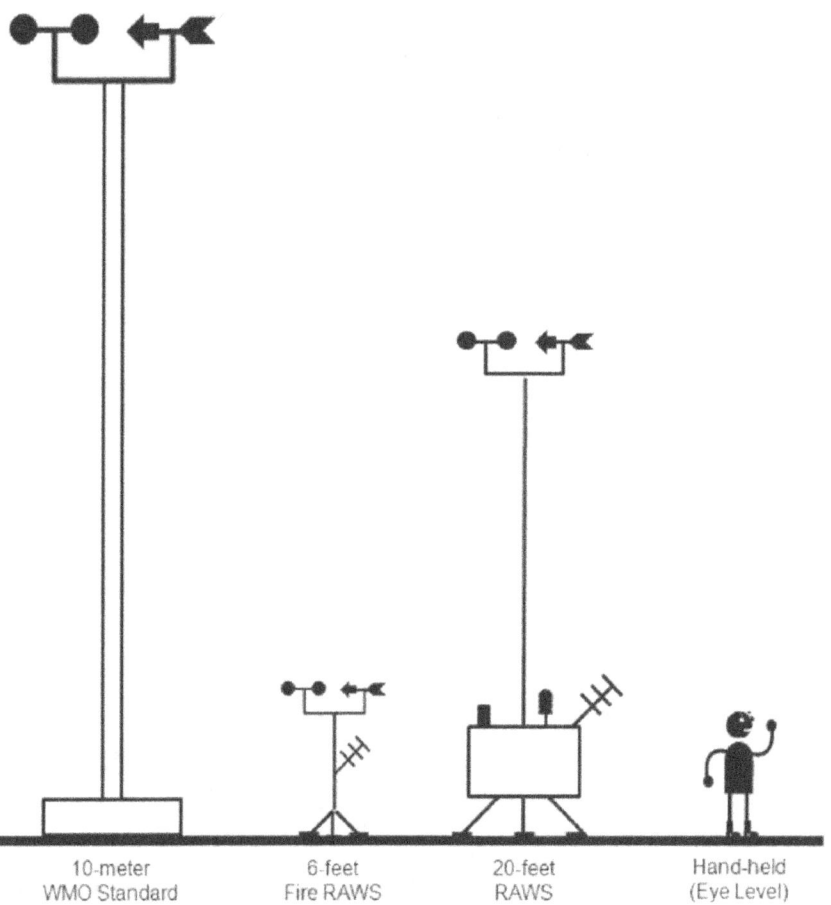

Figure 3—Various height standards are used for wind measurements and forecasts.

This paper describes models and methods for determining WAF. The influence of WAF and of the definition of "midflame height" on fire model results is demonstrated. The vertical difference in wind velocity can be significant. Midflame wind speed may be only 10 percent of the wind speed 20 ft above the tree tops. Of the many variables related to wind speed as it affects fire behavior, this report addresses only the vertical adjustment of a single wind velocity value. Wind adjustment factor does not address the effect of landscape on 20-ft wind speed and direction, nor does it deal with the various time averaging methods.

An effective user of wildland fire modeling systems is aware of model assumptions and of the effect of user selections on results. While it is possible to use models as a black box, it is not recommended. This report will be useful to those who desire an understanding of the modeling behind wind adjustment factor and midflame wind speed at a technical level. In addition to interested practitioners and course developers, the intended audience consists of system developers, analysts, meteorologists, and researchers. Developers of fire modeling systems and methods should make informed decisions on how to include midflame wind and WAF. An analyst who is comparing predicted and observed fire behavior should be aware of the influence of the method of determining wind speed for the calculations. Meteorologists who have a basic understanding of how fire models use midflame wind speed and wind adjustment factor can potentially provide better fire weather forecasts. Researchers who are working on new fire behavior models can recognize limitations of current methods and develop improvements for the future.

It is assumed that the reader is familiar with fire modeling concepts and terminology (for example, Rothermel 1983) and with the BehavePlus fire modeling system (Andrews 2007; Heinsch and Andrews 2010). BehavePlus is used as the basis for description of WAF and midflame wind speed and their effect on modeled surface fire behavior. Details of the WAF models (equations) as implemented in BehavePlus are also given. This is followed by a description of the use of WAF in other applications, such as FARSITE, NFDRS, and the Fireline Handbook (NWCG 2006), with comparison to the method used in BehavePlus. In the final section of this report, we discuss the limitations of WAF models and the need for additional research and development.

Rothermel's Surface Fire Spread Model

Fire Model Development

Because midflame wind and WAF are meaningful only in the context of Rothermel's surface fire spread model, we begin with relevant points on development of the model. The spread model is based, in part, on experimental burns in a wind tunnel and on a data set of fast spreading wildfires. The final model describes the wind input as "mean wind speed at midflame height" (Rothermel 1972: p.33).

Laboratory facilities allow the study of fires in a controlled environment, which is not possible in the field. Combustion facilities were designed to control airflow uniformly within the test areas. This means uniformity of the average flow across the test area as well as of the velocity fluctuations within the average flow (Rothermel 1965, 1967). Data were collected with mean wind tunnel velocity set at 2, 4, 6, or 8 mi/h (Rothermel 1972; Rothermel and Anderson 1966). The wind velocity was therefore not related to the height of the flames, but was the average value for the uniform flow in the wind tunnel.

In order to expand the range of conditions beyond what was possible in the laboratory, Rothermel also used a data set from fast spreading grass fires in Australia (McArthur 1969). Fifteen data points provided forward rate of spread for "average wind velocity at 33' in the open" (10-m wind). Specific fuel data were not available; fuel bed depth was assumed to be 1 ft. While not specifically stated, a comparison of figure 19 and figure 20 in Rothermel (1972) indicated that 10-m wind was multiplied by 0.4 to estimate midflame wind. (This is equivalent to WAF of 0.46 for 20-ft wind.)

It is not technically possible to define the height of midflame wind in the field in terms that match the data used for fire model development. As is the case for all models, developing WAF models involves assumptions and simplifications, which are described in this report.

Midflame Wind

While the term "midflame" wind indicates the wind at the midpoint of the flame, that is not a precise definition. The fire model was developed to use information available before the fire burns (Rothermel 1972). Midflame wind speed is the average wind velocity that affects surface fire spread. The term "midflame" was coined to make the distinction between the "free wind" at 20 ft or 10 m above the vegetation and the reduced wind that is used in calculating surface fire spread rate. Because it was defined specifically for Rothermel's surface fire spread model, the term "midflame" applies only to surface fire, not crown fire.

If the height for the wind velocity depended specifically on flame height, then a calculation of flame height would be needed to determine the wind speed used in the calculation of flame height. This would not be acceptable and is not the case. The model for WAF is based on fuel bed depth, while the flame height for fires in fuel of that depth can vary significantly based on fuel moisture, wind speed, and slope. According to Rothermel (1983), "The model is complete in the sense that no prior knowledge of a fuel's burning characteristics is required. All that is necessary are inputs describing the physical and chemical makeup of the fuel and the environmental conditions in which it is expected to burn…. Environmental inputs are mean wind velocity and slope of terrain."

Weather measurements taken on-site with a belt weather kit or other hand-held device are at eye level. This is an appropriate estimate of midflame wind, as described by Rothermel (1983). He cautions that the location of the measurements must be reconciled with the fire location, with consideration of topography, sheltering, and time of day.

Rothermel (1983: preface) stated that it took 10 years to develop the spread model and another 10 years to learn how to obtain the inputs and interpret the outputs for field application. Development of concepts and models for wind adjustment factor to convert 20-ft wind speed to midflame wind speed is one of the steps taken to make the spread model useful for field applications.

Wind Adjustment Factor (WAF) Models

In some cases, a value for midflame wind speed can be used directly to calculate surface fire behavior. In other cases, the wind at 20 ft (or at 10 m) must be converted to an appropriate midflame value. Models for wind adjustment factor are based on a log wind profile, surface fuel depth, and sheltering from overstory vegetation at the site. The model gives an average wind adjustment over a height range, not at a specific height above the ground. WAF tables based on those models are an alternative to direct use of the model calculations. In selecting an appropriate WAF value from a table, a user can consider

factors not in the models, such as the effect of surrounding vegetation as well as the potential of wind to penetrate the overstory due to location on the terrain (for example ridge top versus valley bottom). WAF models and methods address only the vertical adjustment of 20-ft wind speed to midflame wind speed. The effect of terrain on 20-ft wind speed is a separate topic.

Albini and Baughman (1979) developed the modeling foundation for WAFs for wildland fire. In their introduction, they noted the problem with the definition of midflame height: "The poorly defined 'midflame' windspeed can be approximated by using a spatially averaged value of the windspeed over an appropriate height range." Their work dealt only with the steady, undisturbed windfield and its influence on fire in surface fuels. No account was taken of wind direction or the influence of the fire on the wind speed. Furthermore, flat terrain and uniform continuous vegetation cover were assumed.

Albini and Baughman (1979) presented mathematical models for wind characteristics above a vegetative cover that is a single-stratum fuel (grass, brush, etc.) and for wind under a forest canopy. There are two models, one for sheltered and one for unsheltered WAF. We use the term "unsheltered from the wind" rather than "exposed to the wind" to avoid confusion with characterization of understory exposure to the sun in discussing fuel moisture.

While the work of Albini and Baughman (1979) is appropriately listed as a reference for most applications of WAF, there are differences in implementation that are described in this report.

WAF and Midflame Wind in Fire Modeling Systems

The original implementation of the Rothermel surface fire spread model was in the 1972 NFDRS (Deeming and others 1972). Observed 20-ft wind speeds from fire weather stations (Fischer and Hardy 1972) and forecasted winds were reduced to midflame wind speed for the calculation of fire danger indices using a WAF of 0.5 for all nine fuel models. The updated 1978 NFDRS assigned a WAF to each of the 20 fuel models (Deeming and others 1977).

The Rothermel model was first available for fire behavior applications in the FIREMOD program (Albini 1976a) and the nomographs (Albini 1976b). In FIREMOD, midflame wind speed was the required input. The nomographs for the 13 fuel models (Anderson 1982) were initially based on the assumption that wind speed at midflame height was half of the 20-ft wind speed. They were later revised to be based on midflame wind speed rather than 20-ft wind speed to allow for variable WAF (Rothermel 1983). A reformatted set of nomographs that includes an additional 40 fuel models (Scott and Burgan 2005) was also based on midflame wind speed (Scott 2007).

Baughman and Albini (1980) developed the original WAF tables for the 13 standard fire behavior fuel models. The authors included guidance on selection of sheltered versus unsheltered values based on the effect of topography, for example "fuels on high ridges where trees offer little shelter from wind." The table was changed for presentation in the S-590 Advanced Fire Behavior course, as described by Rothermel (1983). Other versions of WAF tables are available in the Fireline Handbook (NWCG 2006), in the nomograph publication (Scott 2007), and in the BehavePlus Help system.

The first computerized fire modeling system to include calculation of an unsheltered wind adjustment factor was the TSTMDL (test model) program of the BEHAVE fire behavior prediction and fuel modeling system (Burgan and Rothermel 1984). The fuel modeling portion of BEHAVE provided a means of developing custom fuel models to meet needs not satisfied by the 13 standard fuel models.

The FARSITE fire area simulator was an early geospatial implementation of Rothermel's surface fire spread model and continues to be widely used. The input data layer of 20-ft wind is automatically adjusted to midflame wind based on surface fuel bed depth and overstory values for each pixel. The WAF calculation method in FARSITE is also used in FlamMap (Finney 2006), FSPro (Finney and others 2010), and FPA.

The BehavePlus fire modeling system offers the option of direct entry of midflame wind speed or of entering 20-ft (or 10-m) wind speed and either entering or calculating WAF. The focus of this report is WAF modeling in BehavePlus followed by a description of other implementations.

Use of models for fire behavior prediction initially relied on use of nomographs (nomograms) and tables and on expert opinion on using appropriate values. The target user was an experienced fire behavior analyst who was able to choose a WAF by considering not only vegetation conditions at the site, but surrounding vegetation and terrain. That approach, however, is not feasible for geospatial modeling systems that necessarily rely on calculated WAF values.

Variation in fuel bed depth, stand characteristics, flame length and height, and wind speed and direction can be more important influences on fire behavior than the WAF. Nevertheless, modeling of fire behavior requires a repeatable method of calculating WAF based on a description of the fuel and vegetation (not on anticipated flame length or height).

Influence of Wind Adjustment Factor

Example runs using BehavePlus illustrate the influence of WAF on fire behavior modeling. (Specifics of WAF determination are given in following sections.) English units match the source documents of Albini and Baughman (1979) and Baughman and Albini (1980). BehavePlus also allows the use of metric units.

The first example (figure 4) shows calculated surface rate of spread and flame length for three values of WAF, for a fire on flat ground in fuel model 2 with 5 percent dead fuel moisture, 75 percent live fuel moisture, and a range of 20-ft wind speeds. Fuel model 2 is a grass type that can be an appropriate choice for an open ponderosa pine stand with annual grass understory or scattered sage within grasslands (Anderson 1982). WAF of 0.2 would be used for fuel that is sheltered from the wind by overstory. WAF of 0.4 would be used if there is no overstory, leaving the surface fuel unsheltered from the wind. A high WAF value of 0.7 (low wind reduction) is also included for comparison. For this example, a 20-ft wind of 12 mi/h results in midflame wind speed of 2.4 mi/h under the canopy and 4.8 mi/h in the open. The calculated rate of spread is three times as high in the open (37.9 ch/h) as under the canopy (12.5 ch/h). For a 20 mi/h 20-ft wind, rate of spread using WAF of 0.7 is 253 ch/h, which is much higher than the 93 ch/h based on an appropriate WAF of 0.4 for unsheltered fuels. The influence of WAF on flame length is similar. Plots show calculated rate of spread and flame length for the three WAF values for 20-ft wind speeds from 4 to 20 mi/h.

When modeled fire behavior is used in support of fire management decisions, due attention should be given to WAF. As with all aspects of modeling, the user is responsible for understanding model assumptions and limitations, selecting proper input, and interpreting and applying results appropriately.

Prescribed fire objectives, for example, might include an acceptable level of tree mortality. The mortality models in BehavePlus are based, in part, on scorch height, which is a function of flame length, which is, in turn, dependent on midflame wind speed. Midflame wind can be estimated from 20-ft wind using models for WAF that depend on the sheltering of the wind by the overstory.

USDA Forest Service Gen. Tech. Rep. RMRS-GTR-266. 2012

5

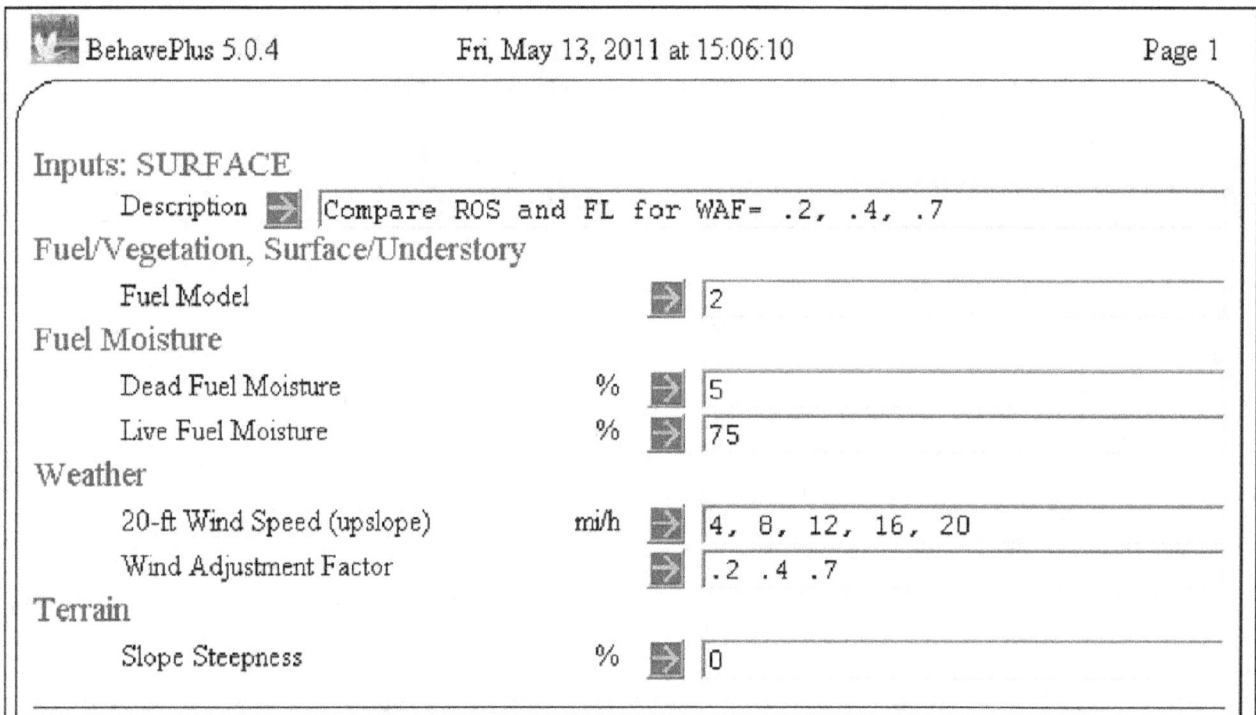

Inputs: SURFACE

Description ➡ Compare ROS and FL for WAF= .2, .4, .7

Fuel/Vegetation, Surface/Understory

Fuel Model ➡ 2

Fuel Moisture

Dead Fuel Moisture % ➡ 5

Live Fuel Moisture % ➡ 75

Weather

20-ft Wind Speed (upslope) mi/h ➡ 4, 8, 12, 16, 20

Wind Adjustment Factor ➡ .2 .4 .7

Terrain

Slope Steepness % ➡ 0

Midflame Wind Speed (upslope) (mi/h)

20-ft Wind mi/h	Wind Adjustment Factor		
	0.2	0.4	0.7
4	0.8	1.6	2.8
8	1.6	3.2	5.6
12	2.4	4.8	8.4
16	3.2	6.4	11.2
20	4.0	8.0	14.0

Surface Rate of Spread (maximum) (ch/h)

20-ft Wind mi/h	Wind Adjustment Factor		
	0.2	0.4	0.7
4	3.9	7.3	15.8
8	7.3	19.4	49.4
12	12.5	37.9	101.0
16	19.4	62.4	169.2
20	27.9	92.6	253.2

Flame Length (ft)

20-ft Wind mi/h	Wind Adjustment Factor		
	0.2	0.4	0.7
4	2.3	3.1	4.4
8	3.1	4.9	7.5
12	4.0	6.6	10.4
16	4.9	8.3	13.2
20	5.7	10.0	15.9

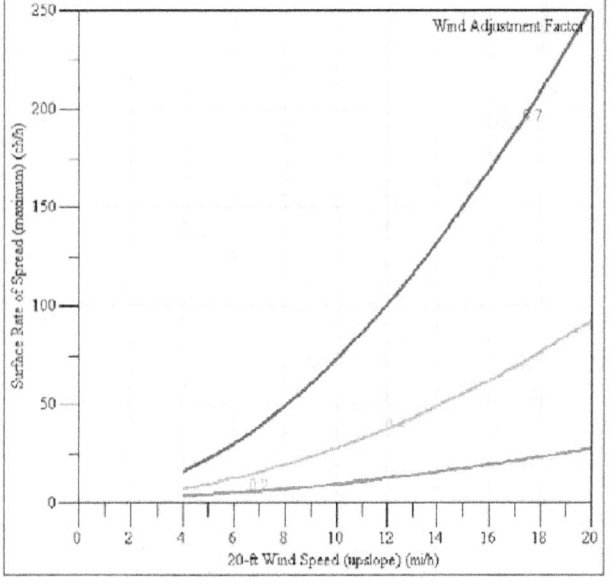

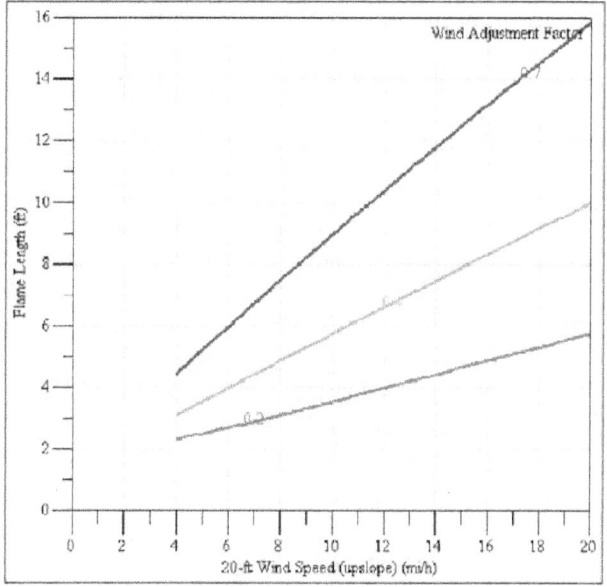

Figure 4—BehavePlus run showing the effect of WAF of 0.2 (sheltered fuel), 0.4 (unsheltered fuel), and 0.7 (a high value for comparison) on calculated surface rate of spread and flame length.

The BehavePlus run in figure 5 illustrates the sheltering effect of overstory and the resulting fire behavior. (A modeler should realize that a change in overstory would also affect fire behavior in other ways, such as a change in fine dead fuel moisture due to a change in exposure to the sun.) The calculated flame length and scorch height are based on the same fuel model and fuel moisture. The effects of three values of canopy cover are shown in the resulting WAFs. In this example, fuels are sheltered from the wind for 40 and 80 percent canopy cover, but are unsheltered at 20 percent cover. At 20 percent cover, the models show 80 percent mortality compared to only 7 percent mortality at 80 percent cover.

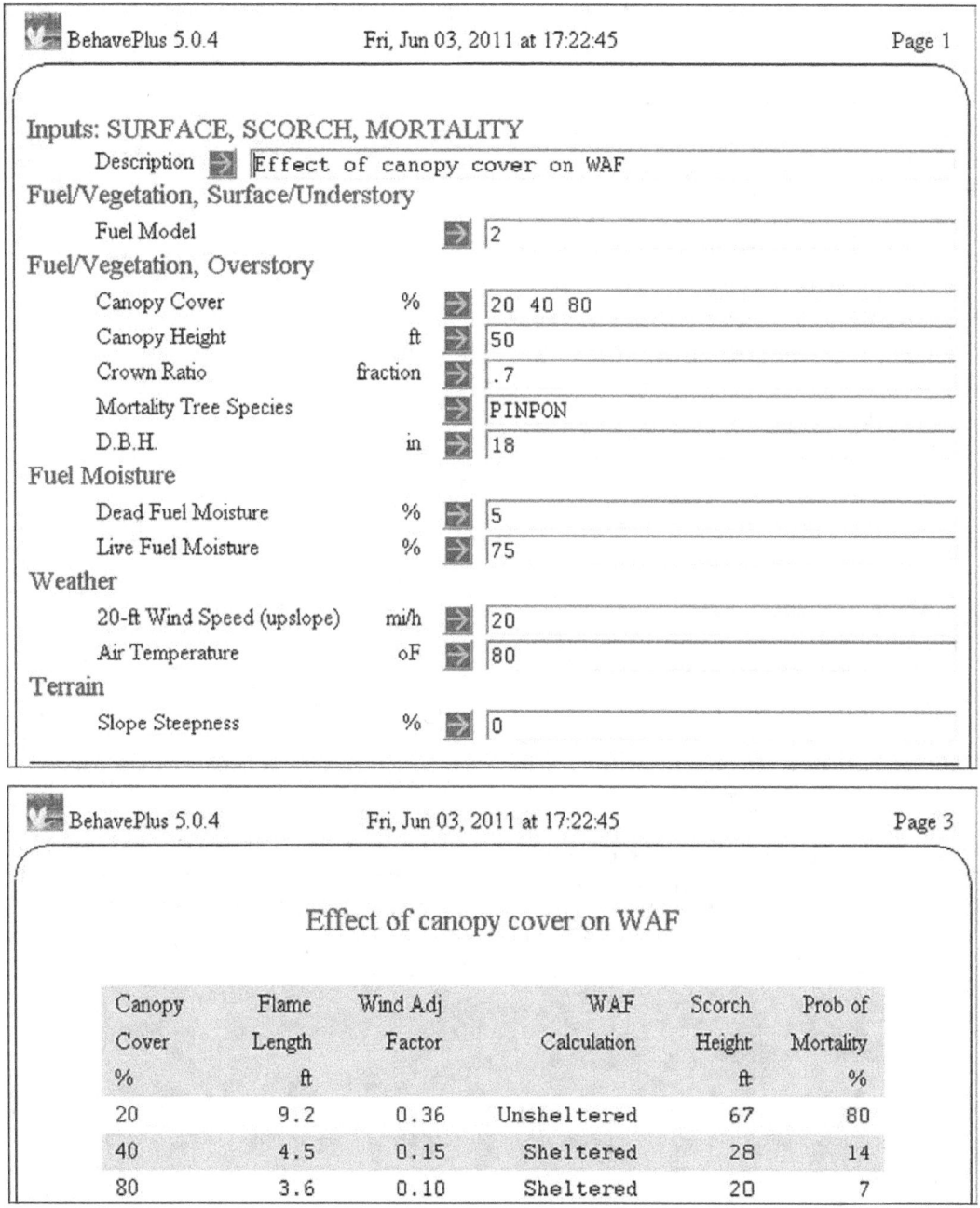

Figure 5—Canopy cover affects calculated WAF, which affects flame length and scorch height, and, ultimately, probability of mortality.

USDA Forest Service Gen. Tech. Rep. RMRS-GTR-266. 2012

7

Equations to Calculate WAF in BehavePlus

This section of the report is a documentation of the mathematical models used to do the calculations in BehavePlus. Complete model development can be found in the referenced publications.

WAF models in BehavePlus are based on the work of Albini and Baughman (1979) and Baughman and Albini (1980), using some assumptions made by Finney (1998). There are separate models for wind above surface fuel that is unsheltered from the wind by overstory and for wind that is sheltered by a forest canopy. Both models are based on a logarithmic wind profile. The unsheltered WAF is based on an average wind speed from the top of the fuel bed to a height of twice the fuel bed depth. The sheltered WAF is based on the assumption that the wind speed is approximately constant with height below the top of a uniform forest canopy. Sheltered WAF is based on the fraction of crown space occupied by tree crowns. The unsheltered WAF model is used if crown fill portion is less than 5 percent. Midflame wind speed is 20-ft wind multiplied by the WAF.

Following are the equations used in BehavePlus. Background and explanation are in following sections.

The unsheltered WAF is

$$WAF = \frac{1.83}{\ln\left(\frac{20 + 0.36H}{0.13H}\right)} \qquad [1]$$

where

H = fuel bed depth, ft

The sheltered WAF is

$$WAF = \frac{0.555}{\sqrt{fH}\ln\left(\frac{20 + 0.36H}{0.13H}\right)} \qquad [2]$$

$f = F \cdot CR$ = fraction of the volume under the canopy top that is filled with tree crowns (crown fill portion)

$F = CC/3$ = fraction of the canopy layer filled with tree crowns

CC = canopy cover, fraction

CR = crown ratio, fraction

The sheltered WAF model is used if crown fill portion (f) is greater than 5 percent.

Log Wind Profile

The WAF models are based on the vertical distribution of wind speed. Albini and Baughman (1979) determined the wind speed above a vegetative cover using the logarithmic wind profile in the following form (Sutton 1953; Albini and Baughman 1979: p. 1).

$$\bar{U}_z = \frac{U_*}{K}\ln\left(\frac{z - D_0}{z_0}\right) \qquad [3]$$

where

$\bar{U}$ = average wind speed at height z

U_* = friction velocity

K = 0.4 (the von Kármán constant)

z = height above ground

D_0 = zero-plane displacement

z_0 = roughness length

Values for D_0 and z_0 were determined to be related to the vegetation height H as D_0=0.64H and z_0=0.13H. The wind speed at a height x above the top of the vegetation is then

$$U_{H+x} = \frac{U_*}{K}\ln\left(\frac{H + x - 0.64H}{0.13H}\right) \qquad [4]$$

A universal dimensionless wind profile can be applied to any vegetation, from short grass to tall trees. A plot of relative height [$(H + x)/H$] versus relative wind speed (U_{H+x}/U_H) is shown in figure 6. The dashed line represents an assumed extension of the wind profile into the vegetation cover (as described in the "Sheltered WAF" section) (Baughman and Albini 1980).

The relationship between the wind speed at 20 ft above the vegetation and the wind at the top of the vegetation (Albini and Baughman 1979: p. 3) is

$$\frac{U_H}{U_{20+H}} = \frac{1}{\ln\left(\frac{20 + 0.36H}{0.13H}\right)} \qquad [5]$$

where

U_H = wind speed at the top of the vegetation

U_{20+H} = wind speed at 20 ft above the top of the vegetation

H = vegetation height, ft

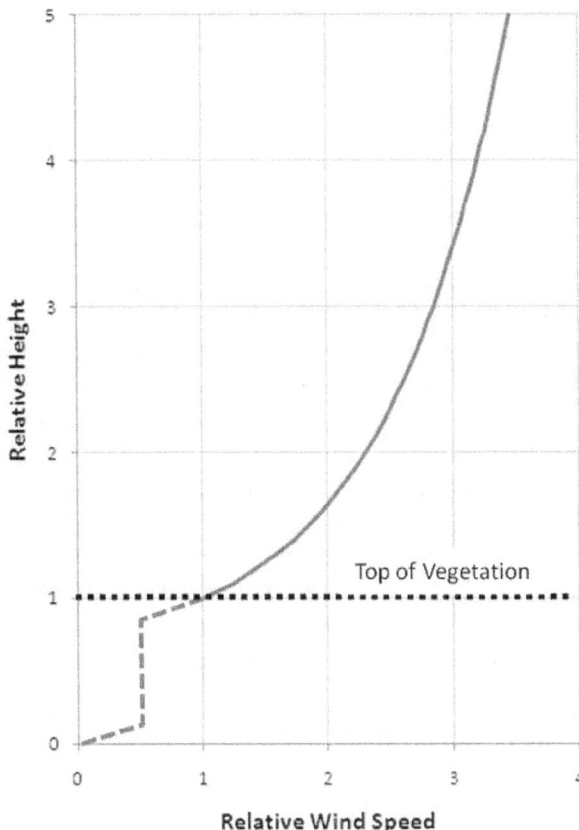

Figure 6—Wind profile (from Baughman and Albini 1980)

Unsheltered WAF

The midflame wind speed over surface fuel that is not sheltered from the wind by overstory is determined by averaging the wind over a height range over the fuel. The average wind speed over the height range from H to $H + H_F$ (Albini and Baughman 1979) is

$$\frac{\overline{\overline{U}}}{U_{20+H}} = \frac{1 + 0.36H/H_F}{\ln\left(\frac{20 + 0.36H}{0.13H}\right)}\left[\ln\left(\frac{H_F/H + 0.36}{0.13}\right) - 1\right] \quad [6]$$

where

$\overline{\overline{U}}$ = average wind speed from to H and H_F

H = surface fuel bed depth, ft

H_F = flame extent above the fuel (from the top of the fuel bed to the top of the flame), ft

Albini and Baughman (1979) gave a plot of various WAFs for flame extensions above the fuel bed as the ratio H_F/H.

Baughman and Albini (1980) used the relationships to develop WAF tables for the 13 standard fuel models, which were described by Anderson (1982). Given that "midflame height" is not well defined, the authors didn't define specific criteria, but in most cases used $H_F = H$ to develop their WAF table. BehavePlus follows the assumption made by Finney (1998) in developing FARSITE, that the flame extension above the fuel bed depth is equal to the fuel bed depth. The curve for $H_F/H = 1$ in figure 7 is the relationship in BehavePlus (see figure 19).

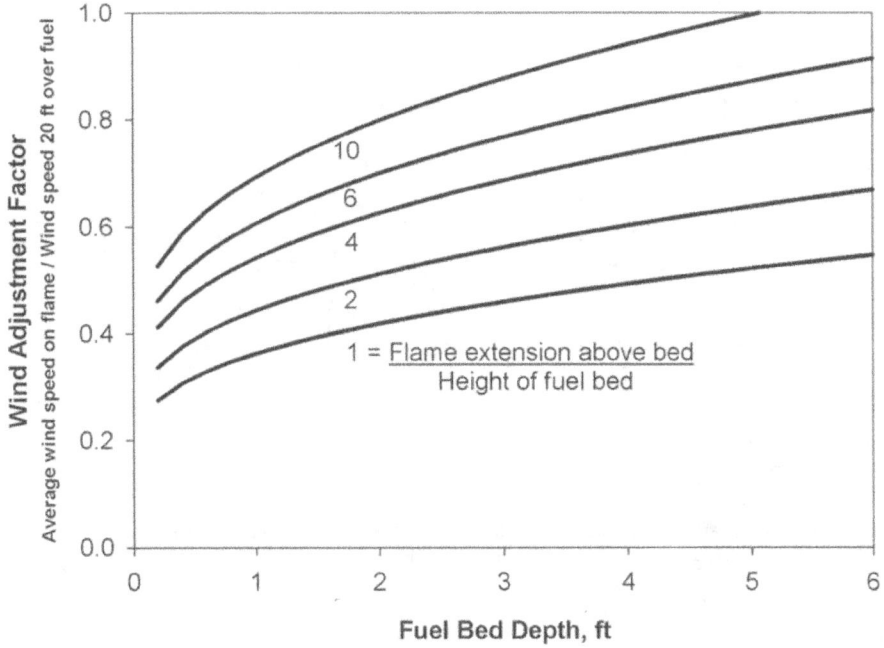

Figure 7—Unsheltered WAF is the average wind speed acting on a flame extending above a uniform surface fuel layer (Albini and Baughman 1979). BehavePlus uses the curve labeled 1, indicating the flame extension above the fuel is equal to the fuel bed depth.

USDA Forest Service Gen. Tech. Rep. RMRS-GTR-266. 2012

9

For $H_F = H$ in equation [6], the unsheltered WAF is calculated as

$$WAF = \frac{\bar{\bar{U}}}{U_{20+H}} = \frac{1.36}{\ln\left(\frac{20 + 0.36H}{0.13H}\right)}\left[\ln\left(\frac{1.36}{0.13}\right) - 1\right] \quad [7]$$

which can be simplified as

$$WAF = \frac{1.83}{\ln\left(\frac{20 + 0.36H}{0.13H}\right)} \quad [8]$$

Figure 8 shows the relationship of fuel bed depth, flame extent above the fuel, flame height, and the height range over which the wind is averaged to find unsheltered WAF.

Sheltered WAF

The sheltered WAF adjusts the wind speed at 20 ft above the top of the overstory vegetation to the wind that influences a fire burning through the surface fuel under a forest canopy.

Albini and Baughman (1979) modeled the variation of wind speed with height for air flow through and under a forest canopy based on the assumption that below some height, near but below the top of the uniform forest canopy, the wind speed is approximately constant with height. Foliage within the live crowns provides a bulk drag force that resists the airflow. The model is based on the portion of volume under the canopy that is filled with tree crowns.

The fraction of the canopy layer filled with tree crowns is F. The canopy layer is measured from the top of the canopy to the bottom of the live crowns. Albini and Baughman (1979) stated that F is approximated by the product of crown cover and a fraction accounting for the tapering of crowns that results in additional void volume higher in the canopy. The authors did not provide a means of calculating F, but used 0.4 for dense stands and 0.1 for open stands.

BehavePlus uses the assumption made by Finney (1998) for FARSITE that the tree crown is conical shaped, the volume of which is one-third that of a cylinder with the same base. BehavePlus does not include the additional factor of $\pi/4$ used in FARSITE to account for the additional void resulting from a square horizontal packing of circular crowns. The fact that an area cannot be filled 100 percent by circles is a minor model limitation compared to the actual variation in overstory.

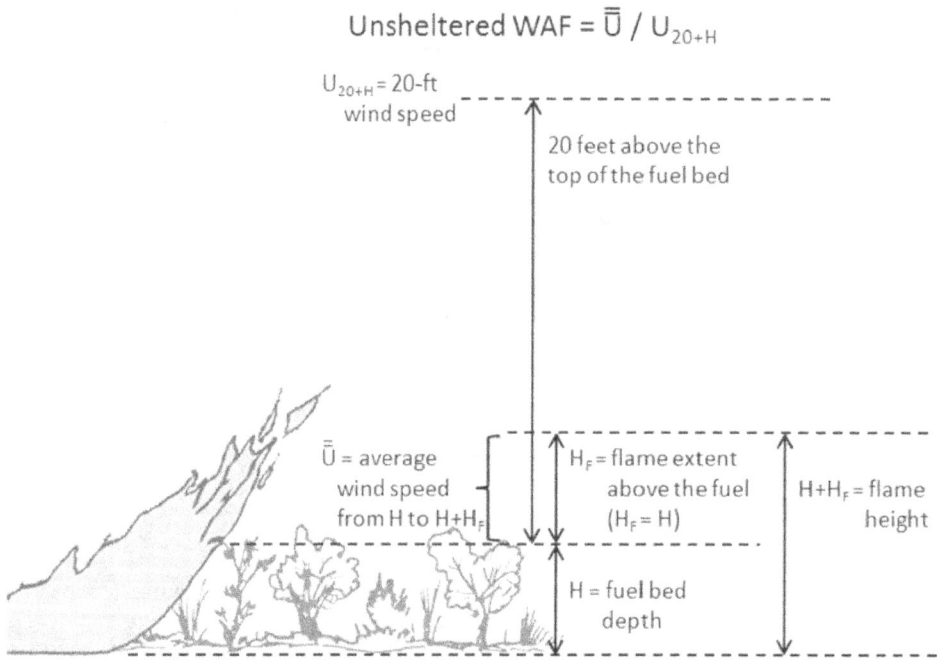

Figure 8—Unsheltered WAF is the average wind speed from the top of the fuel bed to twice the fuel bed depth divided by the wind speed at 20 ft above the top of fuel bed.

The portion of the canopy layer filled with tree crowns (F) is calculated as

$$F = CC/3 \qquad [9]$$

where

CC = fraction canopy cover, horizontal coverage

The portion of volume under the canopy top that is filled with tree crowns (f) includes consideration of crown ratio, as described by Albini and Baughman (1979). (In FARSITE, $f = F$ and $CR = 1.0$.)

$$f = CR \cdot F \qquad [10]$$

where

CR = crown ratio

Table 1 gives values from Albini and Baughman (1979) of tree characterization for sheltering of surface fuels from the wind. For comparison, tables 2 and 3 show the portion of the canopy layer filled with tree crowns (F) and the crown fill portion (f) values calculated in BehavePlus using equations [9] and [10]. The ranges of values are similar.

The ratio of the wind under the canopy U_C to the wind speed at the top of the canopy U_H (Albini and Baughman 1979: p. 8) is

$$\frac{U_C}{U_H} = \frac{0.555}{\sqrt{fH}} \qquad [11]$$

Table 1—Values from Albini and Baughman (1979) for sheltered WAF.

	Shade-tolerant trees				Shade-intolerant trees			
	Young		Mature		Young		Mature	
	Dense	Open	Dense	Open	Dense	Open	Dense	Open
F, fraction of the canopy layer occupied by tree crowns	0.4	0.1	0.4	0.1	0.4	0.1	0.4	0.1
CR, crown ratio, fraction	0.8	0.9	0.6	0.7	0.4	0.7	0.2	0.5
f = F x CR, volume filling fraction (crown fill portion)	0.32	0.09	0.24	0.07	0.16	0.07	0.08	0.05

Table 2—Portion of the canopy layer filled with tree crowns (F) calculated from percent canopy cover (CC), equation [9].

CC	F
20	0.07
40	0.13
60	0.20
80	0.27
100	0.33

Table 3—Crown fill portion (f) values calculated from crown ratio (CR) and percent canopy cover (CC), equations [9] and [10].

f		CC				
		20	40	60	80	100
CR	0.2	0.01	0.03	0.04	0.05	0.07
	0.4	0.03	0.05	0.08	0.11	0.13
	0.6	0.04	0.08	0.12	0.16	0.20
	0.8	0.05	0.11	0.16	0.21	0.27
	1.0	0.07	0.13	0.20	0.27	0.33

USDA Forest Service Gen. Tech. Rep. RMRS-GTR-266. 2012

11

The ratio of wind under the canopy to wind at 20 ft above the canopy top (Albini and Baughman 1979: p. 9) is then

$$WAF = \frac{U_C}{U_{20+H}} = \frac{0.555}{\sqrt{fH}\ln\left(\frac{20 + 0.36H}{0.13H}\right)}$$ [12]

Baughman and Albini (1980) plotted this equation as "ratio of wind speed under canopy (midflame) to wind speed at 20 ft above canopy top" versus "height of uniform canopy top, ft" for three values they labeled "fraction of canopy layer filled with tree crowns." The

plot was based on the f value while, in error, the curves were labeled with a description of F. The curves should be labeled as "portion of volume under the canopy top that is filled with tree crowns." A plot of equation [12] with the corrected curve label is given in figure 9.

An alternate plot of equation [12] shows WAF for a range of f values for several canopy height values (figure 10). The canopy fill portion has a greater influence on the results than does canopy height.

Sheltered WAF is a function of canopy height (CH), canopy cover (CC), and crown ratio (CR). The plot in

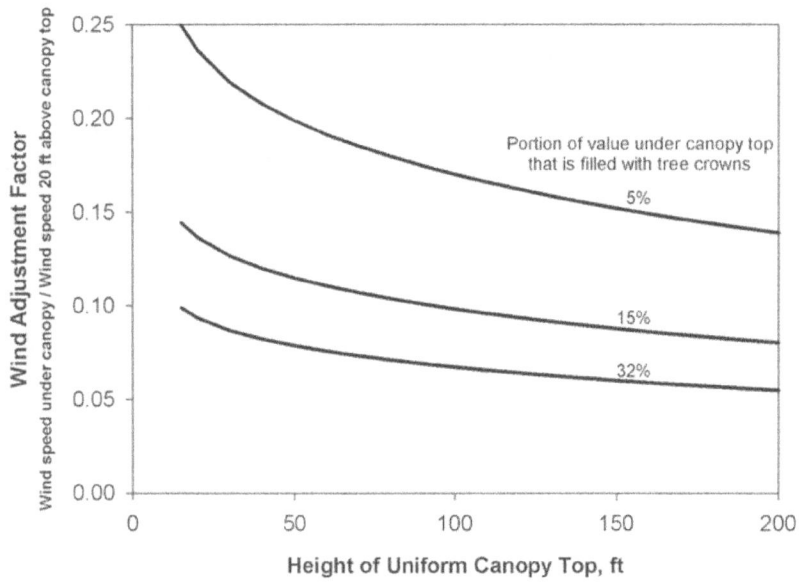

Figure 9—Ratio of wind speed within (and below) forest canopy to wind speed 20 ft above canopy top (adapted from Albini and Baughman 1979).

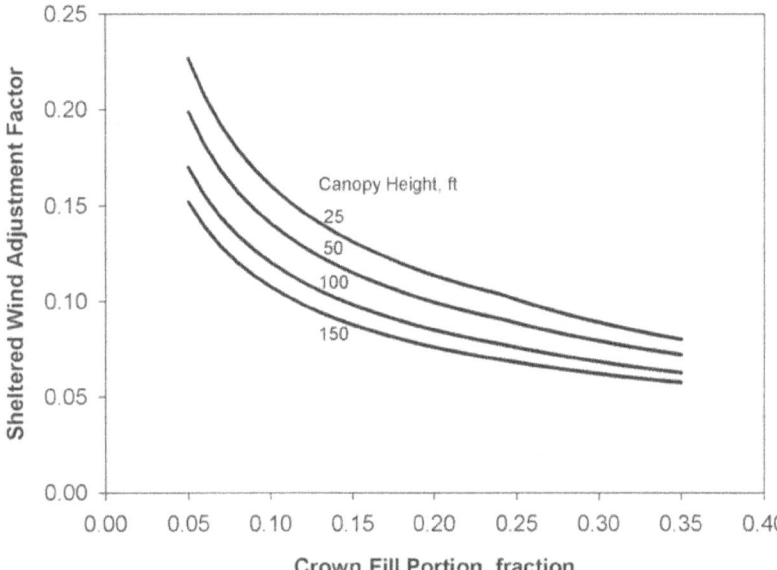

Figure 10—Sheltered WAF for a range of crown fill portion and several values of CH.

figure 11 shows the relationship for *CH* = 100 ft for ranges of *CC* and *CR*. The resulting high WAF values for low canopy cover, especially for low crown ratio, show that it is not appropriate to apply the sheltered model for the full range of values. For an extreme of 1 percent *CC* and 0.2 *CR*, the calculated WAF is 1.66, meaning that midflame wind is greater than 20-ft wind, which is obviously inappropriate. The question is when to use the sheltered versus unsheltered WAF model.

Sheltered Versus Unsheltered

Albini and Baughman (1979) presented two WAF models, one for sheltered fuel and one for unsheltered fuel. The authors did not give specific rules for choosing which model to use, but Baughman and Albini (1980) gave guidance (see figures 17 and 25), which works for tables based on human judgment. However, an explicit rule is needed for computer implementation.

Given a description of the overstory, the question is whether the fuel is sheltered or unsheltered from the wind. Keep in mind that the models are based on the assumption of a uniform canopy on flat ground. A few trees would have little effect and the surface fuel would be considered unsheltered from the wind (figure 12).

For both sheltered and unsheltered conditions, the 20-ft wind is multiplied by the WAF to give midflame wind. Recall that "20-ft wind" is the free wind at 20 ft above the top of the vegetation. That is 20 ft above the top of surface fuel unsheltered from the wind and 20 ft above the tree tops for surface fuels that are sheltered from the wind.

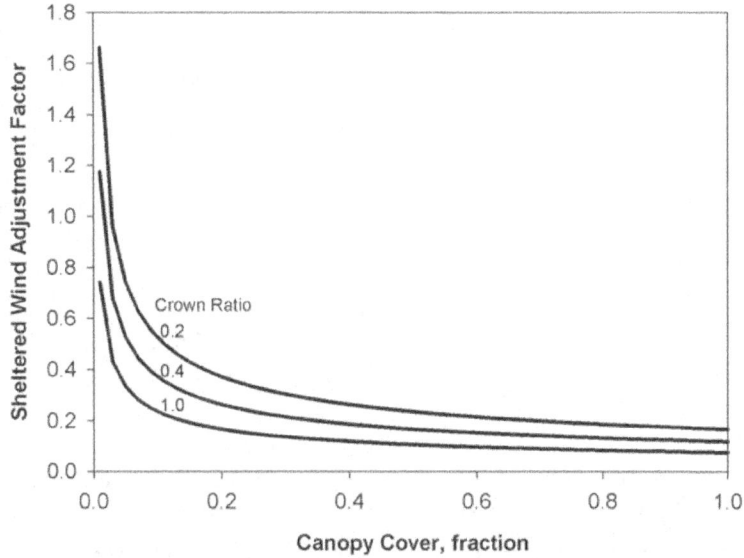

Figure 11—Sheltered WAF for a range of CR and CC, CH is 100 ft. Very low CC values give unreasonably high WAF values. It is therefore not appropriate to use the sheltered model for the entire range of canopy closure values.

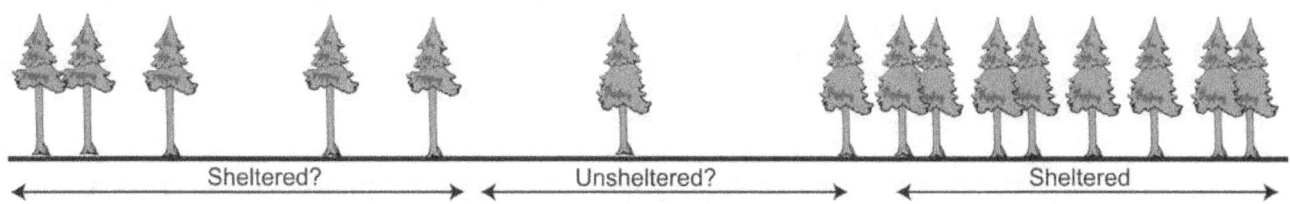

Figure 12—Classification of surface fuel as sheltered or unsheltered depends on the overstory at the site. At some point, the trees have little influence and the fuels are considered unsheltered from the wind.

USDA Forest Service Gen. Tech. Rep. RMRS-GTR-266. 2012

13

Albini and Baughman (1979) gave an example table for crown fill portion (*f*). They described the graph of sheltered WAF (see figure 9) as "plotted for the typical and extreme values of *f*"—5, 15, and 32 percent. Given that the authors considered 5 percent an extreme value for *f*, that value was selected as the cutoff point for the model in BehavePlus. BehavePlus uses a criterion of 5 percent or greater crown fill portion to indicate sheltered conditions. Crown fill portion is determined from both canopy cover and crown ratio.

Figure 13 shows the canopy cover and crown ratio values that result in a crown fill portion (*f*) greater than or less than 5 percent, indicating whether the fuel is considered sheltered or unsheltered. (The FARSITE criterion for sheltered conditions is *CC*>0.)

Definition of Midflame Height

The definition of midflame height has a substantial influence on modeling results. It is not reasonable to base midflame height directly on the height of the flames,

since the objective is to calculate fire behavior from a description of the pre-fire environment, including wind speed. As described above, a consistent method of defining midflame wind to determine a WAF is the average from the top of the fuel bed to twice the fuel bed depth for unsheltered fuel. Because wind is assumed to be constant with height under the canopy, the definition of midflame height is not critical for sheltered conditions.

The definition of midflame wind as the average wind speed over a height range determined by the fuel bed depth, however, cannot be applied to wind measurements, which are taken at a specific height.

In table 4, we compare the calculation of WAF for unsheltered fuel based on the assumption that midflame wind speed is defined as the average wind from the top of the fuel bed to twice the height of the fuel bed (as in BehavePlus and FARSITE) to other definitions of midflame heights. We calculate a WAF for a height twice the fuel bed height, and for heights of 4 ft and 5.5 ft, which might be hand-held (eye level) height for some people. We also look at a 2-m height, which is available on the Oklahoma Mesonet (McPherson and others 2007).

To illustrate the effect of various definitions of midflame height on modeled WAF and fire behavior, consider a fire in fuel model GS2 (moderate load, dry climate grass-shrub) that has a fuel bed depth of 1.5 ft. Look at the unsheltered WAF for various heights, the resulting midflame wind speed for a 20-ft wind of 15 mi/h, and the calculated rate of spread and flame length. For midflame height defined as the height above the ground, use equation [4] for the ratio of ($U_z = U_{x+H}$) to U_{20+H} to find WAF.

In all cases, we use the same fuel model (GS2), fuel moisture (dead 5 percent and live 75 percent), slope (zero), and 20-ft wind (15 mi/h). The average wind from 1.5 to 3 ft above the ground is the definition of midflame wind used in BehavePlus (equation [6]), resulting in a WAF of 0.39, midflame wind speed of 5.9 mi/h, rate of spread of 31 ch/h, and flame length of 5.8 ft. Midflame wind at all other selected heights is higher. At 5.5 ft, WAF is 0.68, midflame wind is 10.2 mi/h, rate of spread is 66 ch/h, and flame length is 8.3 ft.

Figure 14 illustrates values in table 4, showing the log wind profile with the wind speeds at various heights compared to the average wind for the height range used in the WAF model.

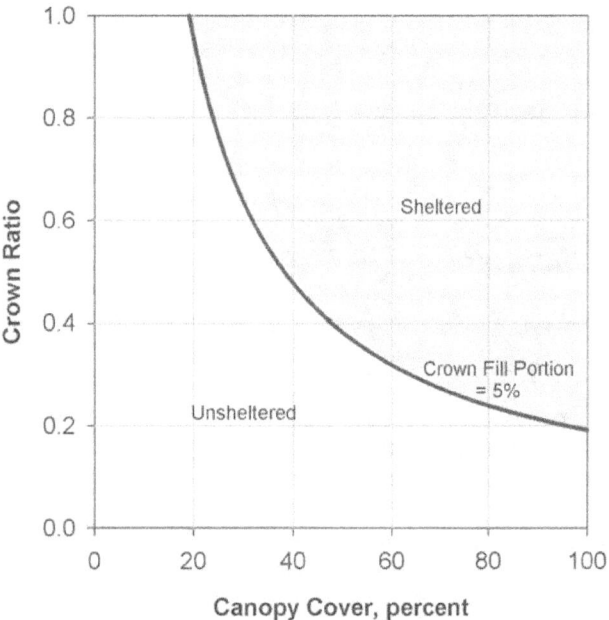

Figure 13—In BehavePlus, the unsheltered WAF model is used for crown fill less than 5 percent.

Table 4—WAF from the definition of midflame wind as the average over a height range based on Albini and Baughman (1979) and used in BehavePlus and FARSITE as compared to other midflame heights based on the same log wind profile, equation [4].

"Midflame" height above ground (fuel bed depth = 1.5 ft)	Height above the fuel, H = 1.5 ft	Calculated WAF (eq. [4])	Midflame wind = WAF x (20-ft wind = 15 mi/h)	Rate of spread[a], ch/h	Flame length[a], ft
1.5 to 3 ft (average from top of fuel to twice the fuel bed depth)	0 to 1.5	0.39	5.9	31	5.8
3 ft (twice the fuel bed depth)	1.5	0.50	7.5	43	6.8
4 ft (shorter person hand-held)	2.5	0.59	8.8	54	7.5
5.5 ft (taller person hand-held)	4.0	0.68	10.2	66	8.3
6.56 ft (2 m)	5.06	0.72	10.8	72	8.6

[a]Fuel model GS2, dead moisture 5 percent, live moisture 75 percent, slope 0 percent

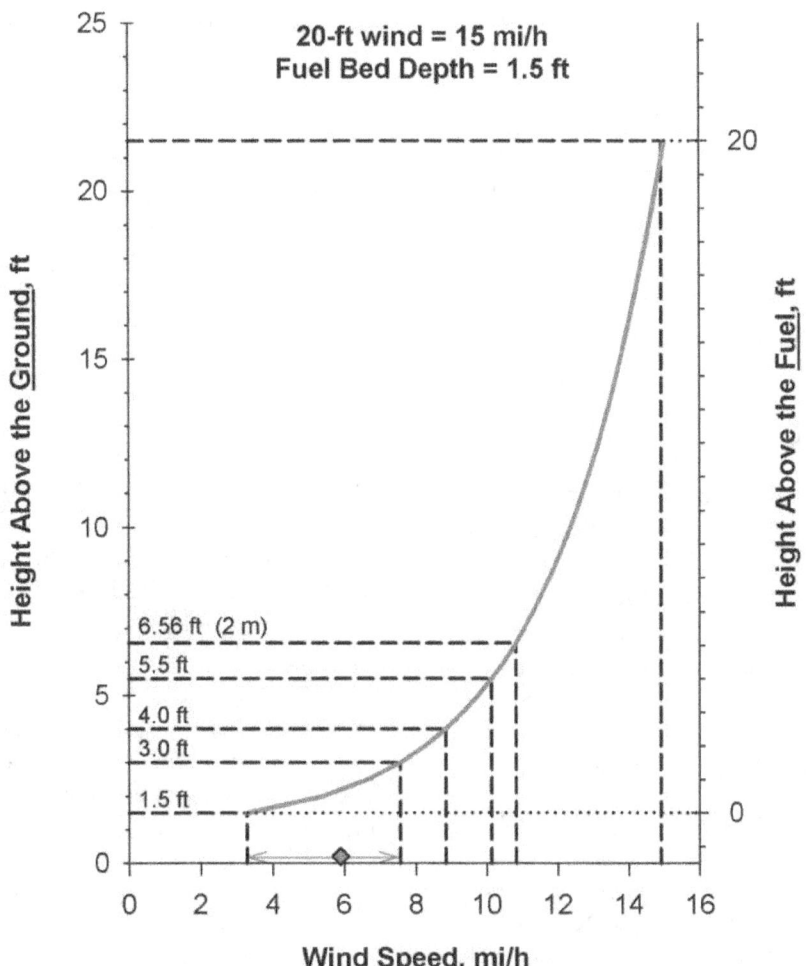

Figure 14—Illustration of height and wind speed values in table 4. For a fuel bed depth of 1.5 ft, WAF is based on an average wind speed from 1.5 to 3.0 ft.

USDA Forest Service Gen. Tech. Rep. RMRS-GTR-266. 2012

15

WAF Implementation in BehavePlus

The BehavePlus fire modeling system integrates many mathematical models for fire behavior, fire effects, and the fire environment, including models for WAF (Andrews 2007). In calculating surface fire behavior, the BehavePlus system's SURFACE module offers three options:

- direct entry of midflame wind speed,
- entry of WAF and 20-ft (or 10-m) wind speed, and
- calculation of WAF for entered 20-ft (or 10-m) wind speed.

Each of these options is applied with examples in the following sections. All are based on 20-ft wind, which is the basis of the WAF models. When a BehavePlus user enters a 10-m wind speed, the value is divided by 1.15 to get 20-ft wind (Turner and Lawson 1978).

Most of the following examples are based on the effect of WAF on calculated surface fire rate of spread and flame length. Those outputs from the SURFACE module can be used as inputs to other modules (Andrews 2009; Heinsch and Andrews 2010). WAF therefore affects scorch height (SCORCH), tree mortality (MORTALITY), transition to crown fire (CROWN), spotting distance from a wind-driven surface fire (SPOT), safety zone size (SAFETY), size of a point source fire (SIZE), and fire containment (CONTAIN).

Midflame Wind Speed

It is common for a user to specify values for midflame wind speed, skipping the step of adjusting 20-ft wind to midflame height. This option is useful for several applications, including the following:

- Calculation of fire behavior from wind speed measured at a site or from a spot weather forecast of eye level wind.
- Exercising the fire spread model to examine sensitivity to input values: wind, slope, fuel, and moisture.
- Comparison of fuel models for a range of wind speeds, as done by Scott and Burgan (2005).
- Examination of fuel treatment options for constant midflame wind speed and fuel moisture.

As is the case with all aspects of fire behavior prediction and use of BehavePlus, the user is responsible for making good decisions. Recognition of the role of WAF cannot be ignored, even when it is neither input nor calculated.

Comparison of fire behavior in two fuel models for a range of midflame wind speeds should include consideration of sheltering effects on the wind. Some fuel models such as fuel model 9, long needle litter, are generally sheltered, while others such as fuel model SH5, high load, dry climate shrub (chaparral), are often unsheltered. In figure 15, we compare the calculated rate of spread for the two fuel models for the same moisture and slope values for a range of midflame wind speed from 0 to 20 mi/h. The plot does compare the role of the fuel models in the mathematical fire model. What might seem like a reasonable midflame wind speed might imply an unrealistic 20-ft wind speed. Midflame wind of 10 mi/h for unsheltered chaparral would be equivalent to a realistic 20 mi/h 20-ft wind (WAF = 0.5). A 10 mi/h midflame wind on a litter fire under a closed canopy would, however, be equivalent to an unreasonable 100 mi/h at 20 ft above a closed canopy (WAF = 0.1). Just because the program lets a user enter a value, it doesn't mean that the value is reasonable or appropriate for fire behavior calculation.

When midflame wind speed is used in the calculations, it is used as specified and is not adjusted according to flame height. Figure 16 shows calculated flame lengths for a midflame wind of 6 mi/h for fuel models SH3 (moderate load, humid climate shrub) and SH6 (low load, humid climate shrub). The calculated flame length for fuel model SH6 is 11 ft at 5 percent dead moisture and 2 ft at 28 percent dead moisture. The same midflame wind speed is used in all cases. Wind speed is not adjusted according to the calculated flame length. Midflame wind is the wind that affects surface fire spread. It is customary to think of eye level wind as midflame wind.

Input WAF

In BehavePlus, if wind is specified at the 20 ft or 10 m height, the WAF can be entered directly. This allows for the use of any WAF values, such as those developed by Norum (1983). Direct entry of WAF permits judgment and consideration of factors not included in the calculations. The original application of WAF was through use of tables and guidelines and relied on expert opinion. That method remains a valid approach when possible.

While calculations are based on a description of the vegetation at the site under the assumption of a uniform canopy cover on flat ground, a person can consider the effect of terrain and non-uniformity on sheltering from the wind. This is appropriate if the objective is to predict the behavior of an ongoing wildfire or to model potential fire behavior for a prescribed fire. While the point modeling in BehavePlus leaves room for the role of expert opinion, geospatial systems such as FARSITE must rely on calculated WAF.

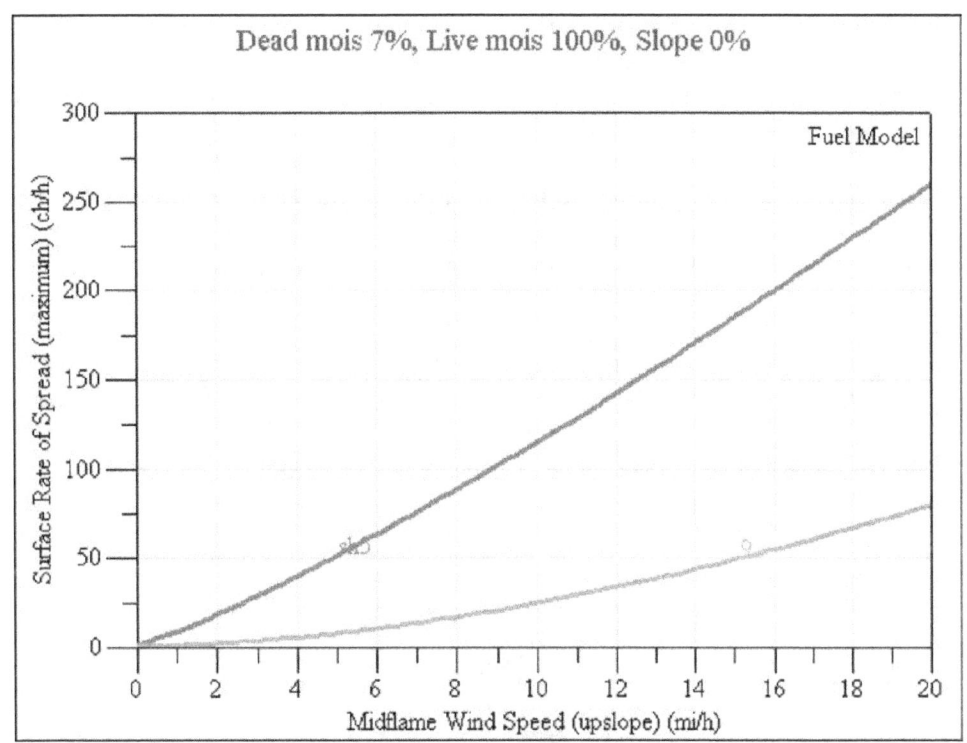

Figure 15—Two fuel models are compared for a range of midflame wind speed. High midflame winds are reasonable for unsheltered shrub fuels (sh5) but not for sheltered litter fuels (9).

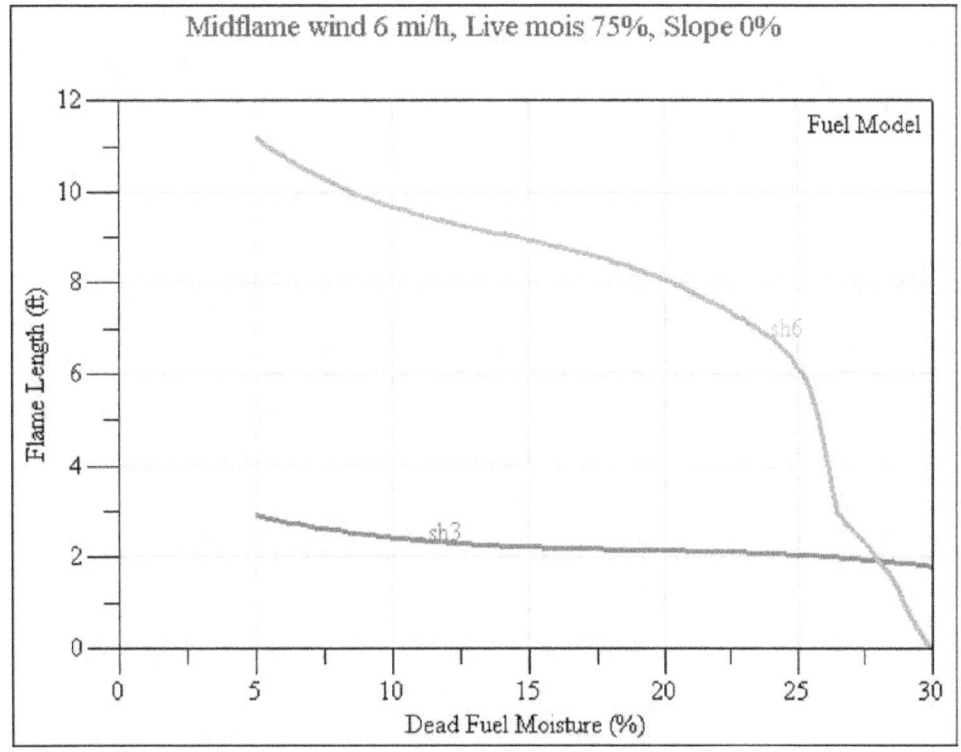

Figure 16—Comparison of flame length for two fuel models for a range of dead fuel moisture values for constant live moisture, slope, and midflame wind speed. The midflame value is as specified and is not adjusted according to the height of the flames.

USDA Forest Service Gen. Tech. Rep. RMRS-GTR-266. 2012

17

WAF tables and guidelines are included in the BehavePlus Help system (figure 17). The table gives the unsheltered WAF for the 53 standard fuel models. The diagram is a visual display of the sheltering conditions given on the table. Even if the canopy is continuous for an area, surface fuel on a ridge top might be unsheltered from the wind. The diagram addresses only adjustment of 20-ft wind to midflame height based on sheltering conditions. It does not relate to the effect of terrain on 20-ft wind.

Figure 4 showed the effect of WAF of 0.2, 0.4, and 0.7 on surface fire rate of spread in fuel model 2. Note on the tables that WAF of 0.2 represents fully sheltered, open stands, and the unsheltered WAF for fuel model 2 (with a fuel bed depth of 1 ft) is 0.4. Note also that none of the WAF on the table is greater than 0.5.

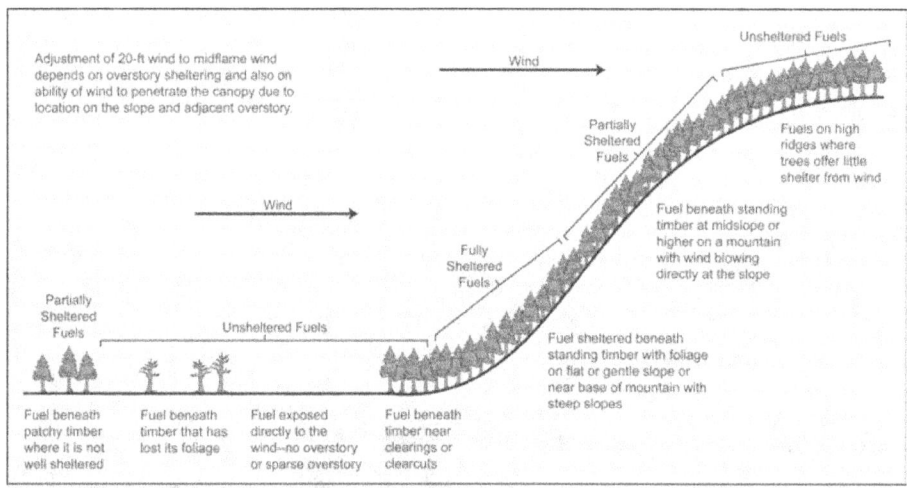

Surface fuel sheltering from the wind	Wind Adjustment Factor (WAF)	Fuel Model
Unsheltered • Surface fuels not sheltered from the wind • No overstory • Sparse overstory • Timber that has lost its foliage • Timber on high ridges where trees offer little sheltering	0.5	• 4, 13 • GR7, GR8, GR9 • SH4, SH5, SH7, SH8, SH9 (depth < 0.9 ft, < 0.3 m)
	0.4	• 1, 2, 3, 5, 6, 7, 10, 11, 12 • GR2, GR3, GR4, GR5, GR6 • GS1, GS2, GS3, GS4 • SH1, SH2, SH3, SH6 • TU2, TU3, TU5 • SB1, SB2, SB3, SB4 (depth 0.9 - 2.7 ft, 0.3 - 0.8 m)
	0.3	• 8, 9 • GR1 • TU1, TU4 • TL1, TL2, TL3, TL4, TL5, TL6, TL7, TL8, TL9 (depth > 2.7 ft, > 0.8 m)
Partially sheltered • Patchy timber • Timber at midslope or higher with wind blowing directly at the slope	0.3	• All fuel models
Fully Sheltered • Standing timber on flat or gentle slope	0.2	• **Open stands.** All fuel models
• Standing timber near base of mountain with steep slopes	0.1	• **Dense stands.** All fuel models

Figure 17—From the BehavePlus Wind Adjustment Factor help window. The diagram illustrates sheltering conditions described on the table. The unsheltered WAF is based on fuel bed depth.

Calculate WAF

BehavePlus offers the option of calculating WAF using the two mathematical models—one for unsheltered surface fuel and the other for surface fuel that is sheltered from the wind by overstory. Whether or not the fuel is sheltered depends on overstory characteristics. The option of calculating WAF is appropriate if the uniformity assumption is valid and if there is need for repeatability based on a model without adjustment for human judgment. In addition, the calculation option can be used to understand the WAF models, as we illustrate in this section.

In the BehavePlus run in figure 18, only WAF was calculated (no fire behavior or fire effects calculations). All 53 standard fuel models were selected and canopy cover was set to zero. The result is unsheltered WAF based on only fuel bed depth. If The BehavePlus output was presented to one decimal place, values would agree with those in the table in figure 17. Note that the unsheltered WAF for fuel model 2 is 0.36, which corresponds to 0.4 on the table in figure 17. The WAF for fuel model 4 is 0.55 in figure 18 and 0.5 in figure 17 because the calculated WAF to three decimal places is 0.547, which rounds to 0.5. Similarly, WAF is 0.547 for fuel models SH5 and SH7 and is 0.447 for SB4.

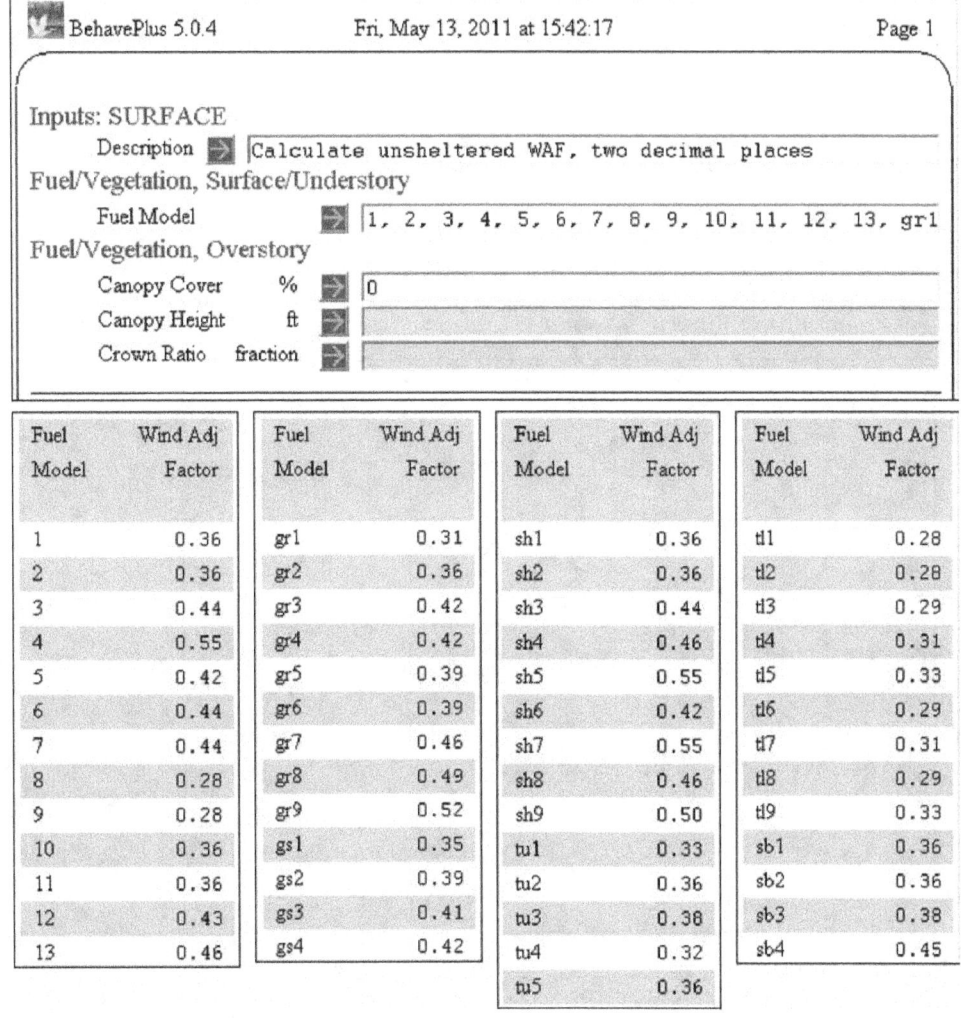

Figure 18—Calculated unsheltered WAF to two decimal places for the 53 standard fuel models.

The BehavePlus run in figure 19 uses the option of the surface fuel description entered as fuel parameters rather than as fuel model. Because BehavePlus is designed to request only relevant input, when only WAF is calculated, the only fuel parameter on the worksheet is fuel bed depth. For canopy cover of zero, the unsheltered WAF is calculated and plotted for a range of fuel bed depths.

The BehavePlus run in figure 20 shows calculated WAF for fuel model 2 for canopy cover of 40 percent, canopy height of 50 ft, and crown ratio values from 0.1 to 0.9. BehavePlus provides intermediate values to allow examination and understanding of the calculations. The table shows that for crown ratio 0.1 and 0.3, the crown fill portion is less than 5 percent, so the unsheltered WAF

is calculated. For crown ratios of 0.5, 0.7, and 0.9, the sheltered model is used. The plot shows the shift from unsheltered to sheltered conditions.

Calculated WAF is based on surface fuel bed depth if there is no or sparse overstory and on a description of the overstory if it exists at the site. There is, therefore, a discontinuity in the results. The switch between sheltered and unsheltered model in BehavePlus occurs at crown fill portion 5 percent.

Recall that the height of the 20-ft wind is 20 ft above the top of the surface fuel for unsheltered fuel or 20 ft above the tree tops (figure 2). The step change is unsettling, but it is a reflection of the modeling foundation and the switch from one model to the other.

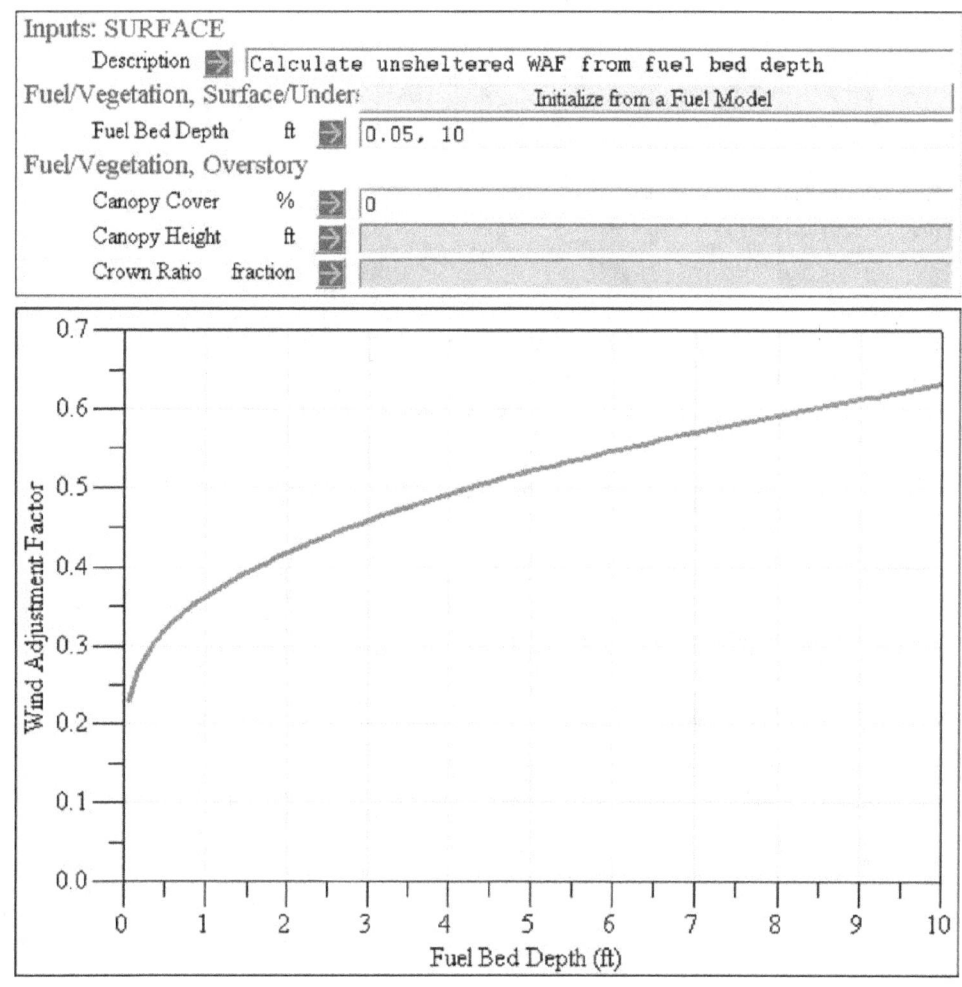

Figure 19—Unsheltered WAF is a function of fuel bed depth.

USDA Forest Service Gen. Tech. Rep. RMRS-GTR-266. 2012

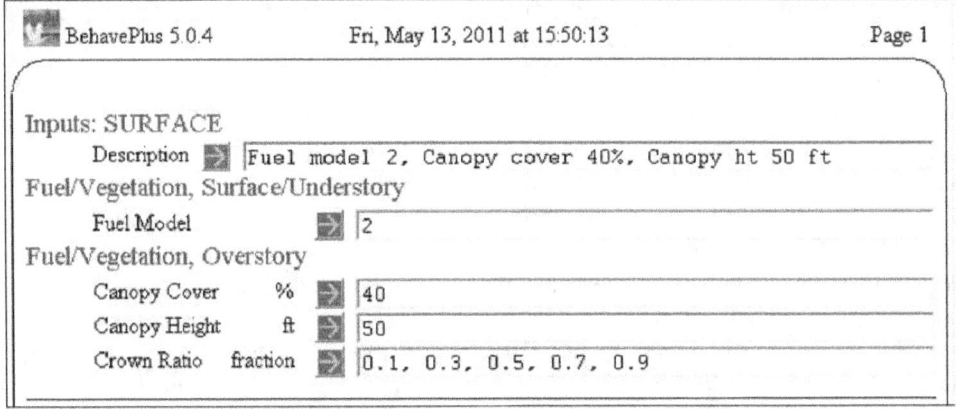

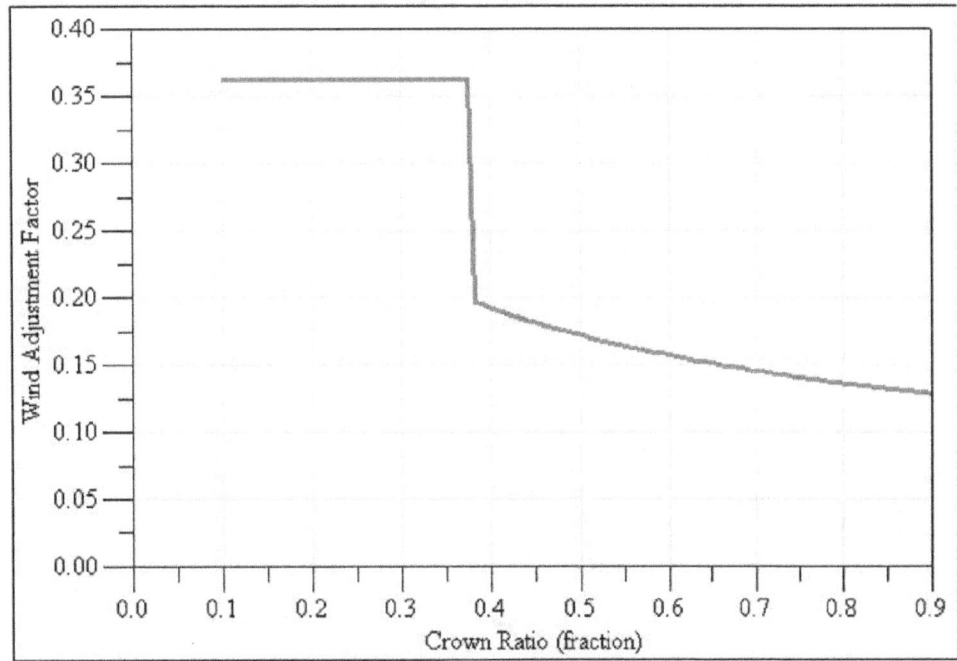

Figure 20—WAF for fuel model 2 for CH of 50 ft, CC of 40 percent, and a range of CR values. Results show the switch between the unsheltered and sheltered WAF models that occurs when crown fill is greater than 5 percent.

USDA Forest Service Gen. Tech. Rep. RMRS-GTR-266. 2012

21

A person using BehavePlus to calculate WAF should look at ranges of values to see when a change in conditions causes the change from sheltered to unsheltered. It is best not to do just a single calculation.

BehavePlus uses a crown fill portion of 5 percent as the indicator of sheltered versus unsheltered fuel. Calculation of crown fill portion is based on canopy cover and crown ratio. Figure 21 is a plot of crown fill portion for canopy cover from 0 to 100 percent for several crown ratio values. A dashed line was added to the BehavePlus plot to indicate 5 percent crown fill. Surface fuel is considered unsheltered from the wind for less than 5 percent crown fill. Note that for crown ratio of 0.1, even for canopy cover of 100 percent, the surface fuel is unsheltered from the wind. For crown ratio of 0.9, fuel is unsheltered for canopy cover less than about 17 percent.

Canopy cover is defined as horizontal coverage. Jennings and others (1999) described the difference between canopy closure and canopy cover. Crown ratio is crown length divided by tree height. Figure 22(a) shows 25 percent canopy cover, and figure 22(b) shows four crown ratios. Each stylized tree in this example has the same base, which would correspond to the same canopy cover.

In figure 23, we look at the effect of canopy cover of 60, 80, and 100 percent, all of which lead to the sheltered case, with crown fill portion greater than 5 percent. Fuel model plays no role in the calculation of sheltered WAF. The plot shows the sheltered WAF for crown ratios of 0.3 to 1.0.

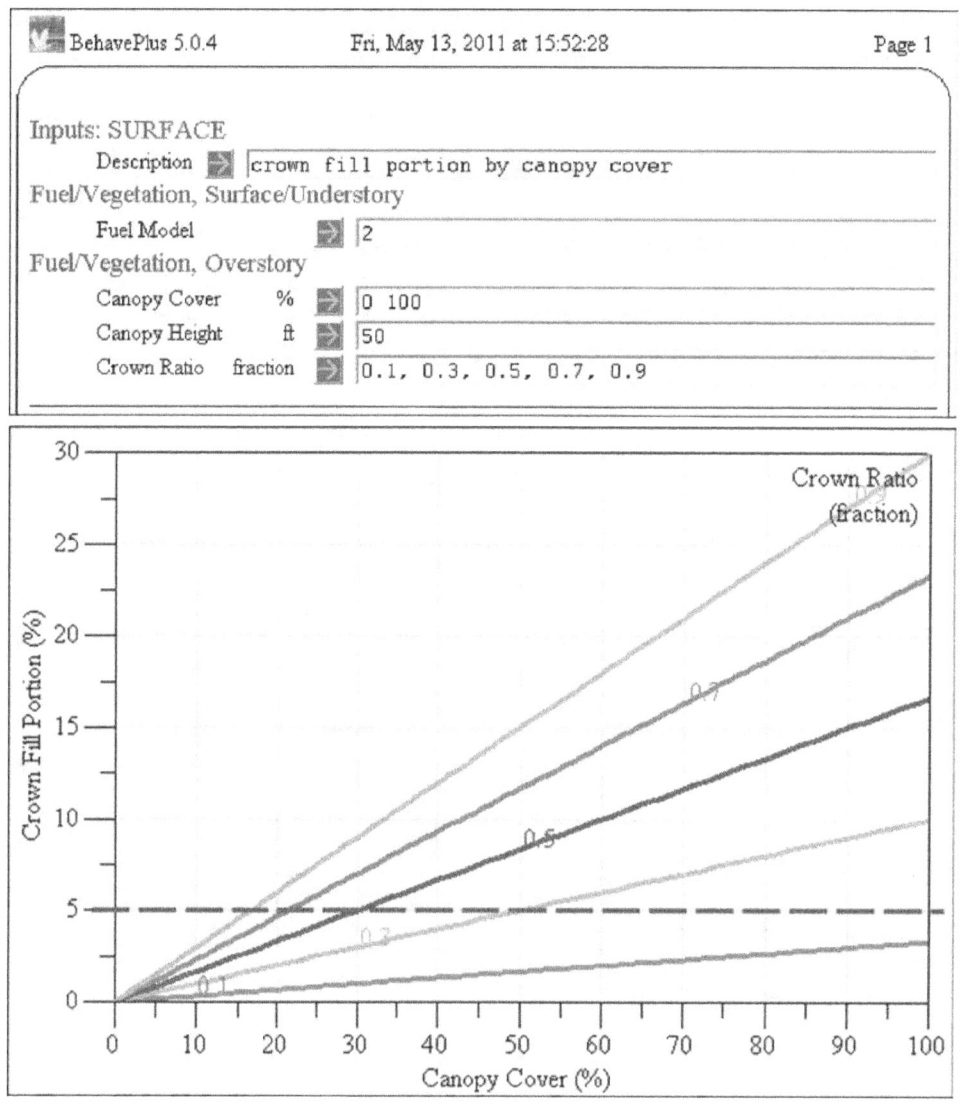

Figure 21—Crown fill portion is a function of canopy cover and crown ratio. Surface fuel is considered unsheltered for crown fill portion less than 5 percent.

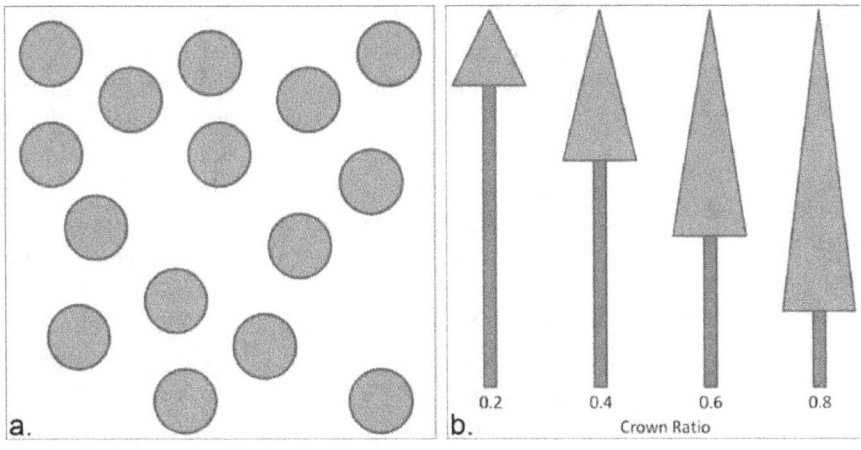

Figure 22—Crown fill portion is a function of canopy cover and crown ratio. (a) CC is horizontal coverage (25 percent in this example). (b) CR is crown length divided by tree height.

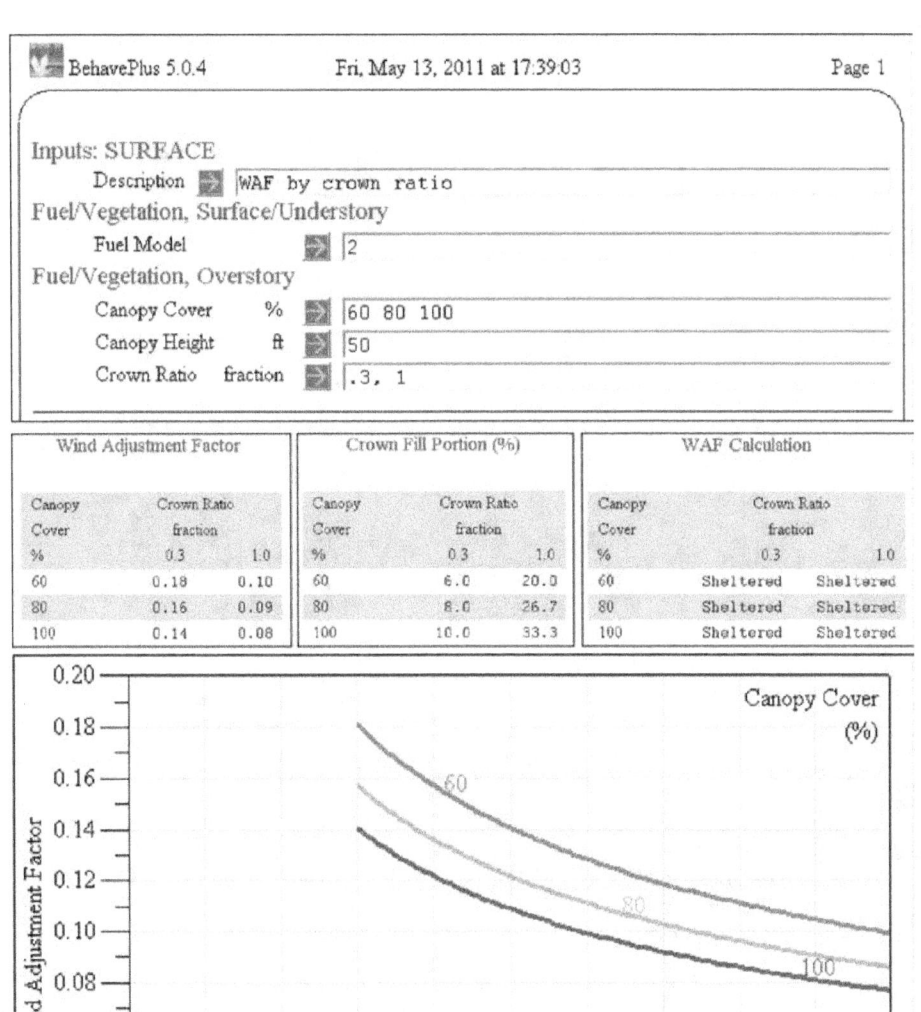

Figure 23—Sheltered WAF is calculated for a range of crown ratios for three values of canopy cover.

USDA Forest Service Gen. Tech. Rep. RMRS-GTR-266. 2012

23

Other Implementations of WAF

WAF modeling in BehavePlus is used as the focus for describing and comparing WAF in other applications. Not all fire modeling systems that include surface fire behavior are included here. FOFEM, for example, requests flame length as input, so it does not request a wind speed to use in calculations (Reinhardt and others 1997). FCCS (Ottmar and others 2007), NEXUS (Scott 1998), and the nomographs (Rothermel 1983; Scott 2007) request midflame wind speed.

WAF Table Comparison

A summary of the differences in WAF table values is given, followed by a description of each application in the following sections.

Table 5 shows the unsheltered WAFs for the 13 standard fire behavior fuel models that were given on various tables compared to those in BehavePlus. The BehavePlus table and Scott (2007) give WAF values for the 53 standard fuel models, while the other sources include only the original 13 fuel models. Inconsistencies are due to differences in calculations and, in some cases, only to rounding.

The sheltered and partially sheltered WAF tables are the same in BehavePlus, Rothermel (1983), and the Fireline Handbook (NWCG 2006). These values are compared in table 6 to those in the original table in Baughman and Albini (1980). Scott (2007) based the sheltered WAF on canopy cover (table 7).

Table 5—Comparison of unsheltered WAF for the 13 standard fire behavior fuel models in several applications.

Fuel model	BehavePlus table	Baughman and Albini (1980)	Rothermel (1983)	Fireline Handbook (NWCG 2006)	Scott (2007)
1	0.4	0.36	0.4	0.4	0.36
2	0.4	0.36	0.4	0.4	0.36
3	0.4	0.44	0.4	0.4	0.44
4	0.5	0.55	0.6	0.5	0.55
5	0.4	0.42	0.4	0.4	0.42
6	0.4	0.44	0.4	0.4	0.44
7	0.4	0.44	0.4	0.4	0.44
8	0.3	0.36	0.4	0.4	0.28
9	0.3	0.36	0.4	0.4	0.28
10	0.4	0.36	0.4	0.4	0.36
11	0.4	0.36	0.4	0.4	0.36
12	0.4	0.43	0.4	0.4	0.43
13	0.5	0.46	0.5	0.5	0.46

Table 6—Comparison of sheltered WAF in several applications.

Shelter from the wind	Baughman and Albini (1980)	BehavePlus, Rothermel (1983), Fireline Handbook (NWCG 2006)
Partially sheltered	0.25	0.3
Fully sheltered, sparse stands, shade-intolerant species	0.17	0.2
Fully sheltered, sparse stands, shade-tolerant species	0.14	0.2
Fully sheltered, dense stands, shade-intolerant species	0.12	0.1
Fully sheltered, dense stands, shade-tolerant species	0.08	0.1

Table 7—Sheltered WAF based on canopy cover from Scott (2007).

Canopy cover, percent	WAF
$5 < CC \leq 10$	0.30
$10 < CC \leq 15$	0.25
$15 < CC \leq 30$	0.20
$30 < CC \leq 50$	0.15
$CC > 50$	0.10

BehavePlus Help System Tables

The unsheltered WAF table in the BehavePlus Help system is generated by the calculations implemented in the program. WAF values are rounded to tenths for the 53 fuel models. The fuel bed depth for each WAF category allows application for custom fuel models (figure 24). (Prior to BehavePlus version 5.0.3, fuel model SH4 was incorrectly listed on the table with WAF = 0.4.) The sheltered values and guidelines are the same as those in Rothermel (1983).

Surface fuel sheltering from the wind	Wind Adjustment Factor (WAF)	Fuel Model
Unsheltered • Surface fuels not sheltered from the wind • No overstory • Sparse overstory • Timber that has lost its foliage • Timber on high ridges where trees offer little sheltering	0.5	• 4, 13 • GR7, GR8, GR9 • SH4, SH5, SH7, SH8, SH9 (depth < 0.9 ft, < 0.3 m)
	0.4	• 1, 2, 3, 5, 6, 7, 10, 11, 12 • GR2, GR3, GR4, GR5, GR6 • GS1, GS2, GS3, GS4 • SH1, SH2, SH3, SH6 • TU2, TU3, TU5 • SB1, SB2, SB3, SB4 (depth 0.9 - 2.7 ft, 0.3 - 0.8 m)
	0.3	• 8, 9 • GR1 • TU1, TU4 • TL1, TL2, TL3, TL4, TL5, TL6, TL7, TL8, TL9 (depth > 2.7 ft, > 0.8 m)
Partially sheltered • Patchy timber • Timber at midslope or higher with wind blowing directly at the slope	0.3	• All fuel models
Fully Sheltered • Standing timber on flat or gentle slope • Standing timber near base of mountain with steep slopes	0.2	• **Open stands.** All fuel models
	0.1	• **Dense stands.** All fuel models

Figure 24—WAF tables from BehavePlus help system.

USDA Forest Service Gen. Tech. Rep. RMRS-GTR-266. 2012

25

Baughman and Albini (1980) Tables

The original WAF table from Baughman and Albini (1980) is shown in figure 25. The authors used the models of Albini and Baughman (1979) for average wind speed over a height range from H to $H+H_F$ (equation [6]) to find an unsheltered WAF for each of the 13 fuel models. The authors did not specifically describe how they reached the 13 values, but stated the following:

> Each midflame windspeed obtained by use of table 3 [Wind reduction table] implies a midflame height. For example, consider a fuel model 3 and the corresponding reduction factor of 0.44. From table 4 [Stylized fuel models], fuel model 3 is found to be 2.5 ft high grass. These values of 0.44 and 2.5 ft are used to enter figure 2 [figure 7 in this paper] where the ratio of the flame height to the fuel bed height is

found to be about 1. Thus the flame height extends about 2.5 ft above the tall grass. The flame height of other fuel models can be found in a similar fashion.

In the above quote, the authors used the term "flame height" to mean the flame extension above the fuel bed (H_F), rather than the distance from the ground to the top of the flame. Baughman and Albini (1980) used flame extension above the fuel bed equal to fuel bed depth ($H_F/H = 1$, $H_F = H$) for all but fuel models 8 and 9. For those fuel models, fuel bed depth is 0.2 ft and the WAF on their table is 0.36. Working backward, as they described, this translates to $H_F/H = 2.5$ and $H_F = 0.5$.

Table 8 is a comparison of WAF values on Baughman and Albini's table (figure 25) to those calculated using equation [6], as is done in BehavePlus (figure 18). There is a difference only for fuel models 8 and 9.

Figure 25—Original WAF table from Baughman and Albini (1980)

Table 8—Unsheltered WAF values for the 13 standard fire behavior fuel models in Baughman and Albini (1980) compared to those calculated in BehavePlus. There is a difference in the results for fuel models 8 and 9 (in bold).

Fuel model	Fuel bed depth, ft	WAF from Baughman and Albini (1980)	WAF Calculated by BehavePlus, eq. [6], for $H_F/H = 1$
1	1.0	0.36	0.36
2	1.0	0.36	0.36
3	2.5	0.44	0.44
4	6.0	0.55	0.55
5	2.0	0.42	0.42
6	2.5	0.44	0.44
7	2.5	0.44	0.44
8	**0.2**	**0.36**	**0.28**
9	**0.2**	**0.36**	**0.28**
10	1.0	0.36	0.36
11	1.0	0.36	0.36
12	2.3	0.43	0.43
13	3.0	0.46	0.46

Rothermel (1983) Tables

The original WAF tables were adjusted for presentation in the S-590 course, as presented in Rothermel (1983) (figure 26). The unsheltered WAF values were based on Albini and Baughman's (1979) unsheltered model (equation [6]). As a means of estimating midflame height, Rothermel (1983) calculated flame height for zero wind and slope and 8 percent dead moisture and 100 percent live moisture for the 13 fuel models. This method was based on the author's statement that "We have found that even though flame length varies considerably with changes in wind speed, flame height is not as variable." He used the calculated flame heights as the flame extension above the fuel bed (H_F) in equation [6].

Rothermel's (1983) calculations and tables are compared to those from BehavePlus in table 9. Rothermel did calculations to hundredths and then used them as guidance for setting WAF values in tenths for the table. Some table values are not strict rounded values from the calculations. For example, the calculated WAF for fuel model 8 of 0.32 is given as 0.4 on the table.

However, the results are similar to those based on the assumption used in BehavePlus (and FARSITE) that flame height (from the ground) is twice the fuel bed depth (flame height = H_F+H). When the WAF calculated in BehavePlus is rounded to tenths, there is a difference between the Rothermel (1983) table and the BehavePlus table for only fuel models 4, 8, and 9. Fuel models 8 and 9 are generally sheltered, so the unsheltered WAF would rarely be used.

Table II-6.— Wind adjustment table. Find the appropriate adjustment factor and multiply it by the 20-ft windspeed. Use the result as the midflame windspeed

Fuel exposure	Fuel model	Adjustment factor
EXPOSED FUELS		
Fuel exposed directly to the wind— no overstory or sparse overstory; fuel beneath timber that has lost its foliage; fuel beneath timber near clearings or clearcuts; fuel on high ridges where trees offer little shelter from wind	4	0.6
	13	0.5
	1,3,5,6,11,12 (2,7)[1] (8,9,10)[2]	0.4
PARTIALLY SHELTERED FUELS		
Fuel beneath patchy timber where it is not well sheltered; fuel beneath standing timber at midslope or higher on a mountain with wind blowing directly at the slop	All fuel models	0.3
FULLY SHELTERED FUELS		
Fuel sheltered beneath standing timber on flat or gentle slope or near base of mountain with steep slopes	All fuel models — Open stands	0.2
	Dense stands	0.1

[1]Fuels usually partially sheltered.
[2]Fuels usually fully sheltered.

Figure 26—WAF table from Rothermel (1983).

USDA Forest Service Gen. Tech. Rep. RMRS-GTR-266. 2012

27

Table 9—Basis of the Rothermel (1983) calculation of unsheltered WAF compared to that used by BehavePlus. There are differences in the results for fuel models 4, 8, and 9 (in bold).

Fuel model	Fuel bed depth (H), ft	Rothermel (1983)				BehavePlus	
		Flame height[a] (F), ft	Flame height/ fuel depth	WAF eq. [6] $H_F = F$	WAF table	WAF table	WAF calculation eq. [6] $H_F = H$
1	1.0	0.99	0.99	0.36	0.4	0.4	0.362
2	1.0	1.6	1.6	0.42	0.4	0.4	0.362
3	2.5	2.7	1.1	0.45	0.4	0.4	0.440
4	6.0	4.9	0.80	0.55	**0.6**	**0.5**	0.547
5	2.0	0.92	0.46	0.35	0.4	0.4	0.418
6	2.5	1.4	0.56	0.37	0.4	0.4	0.440
7	2.5	1.4	0.56	0.38	0.4	0.4	0.440
8	0.2	0.37	1.8	0.32	**0.4**	**0.3**	0.275
9	0.2	0.90	4.5	0.44	**0.4**	**0.3**	0.275
10	1.0	1.6	1.6	0.41	0.4	0.4	0.362
11	1.0	1.1	1.1	0.37	0.4	0.4	0.362
12	2.3	2.7	1.2	0.45	0.4	0.4	0.431
13	3.0	3.7	1.2	0.48	0.5	0.5	0.469

[a]Wind speed 0 mi/h, dead moisture 8 percent, live moisture 100 percent, slope 0 percent. Flame height is used as flame extension above the fuel bed in the WAF model.

The sheltered and partially sheltered values are a simplification of those in Baughman and Albini (1980). A comparison of values was given in table 6.

Fireline Handbook (NWCG 2006) Tables

A table of WAFs is in the Fireline Handbook (figure 27). The sheltered and partially sheltered WAF values are the same as those in BehavePlus and Rothermel (1983), but there are some differences in the unsheltered WAF values. WAF fuel model 4 matches the table in BehavePlus and differs from Rothermel (1983), while the WAF for fuel models 8 and 9 differ from the BehavePlus table and match those in Rothermel (1983).

Scott (2007) Tables

A table of unsheltered WAF values for the 53 fuel models to two decimal places is given in Scott (2007) (figure 28). Those values are based on the same calculation as that used in BehavePlus and match those in figure 18. The BehavePlus Help system table rounds WAF values to tenths and organizes it according to fuel bed depth.

Figure 27—WAF table in the Fireline Handbook (NWCG 2006).

TABLE 7: Wind Adjustment Table		
Fuel Exposure	Fuel Model	Adjustment Factor
UNSHELTERED FUELS: Fuel exposed directly to the wind. No or sparse overstory. Fuel beneath timber that has lost its foliage; fuel beneath timber near clearings or clearcuts; fuel on high ridges where trees offer little shelter form the wind.	4	0.5
	13	0.5
	1, 3, 5, 6, 11, 12	0.4
	{2, 7}[1]	0.4
	{8, 9, 10}[2]	0.4
PARTIALLY SHELTERED FUELS: Fuel beneath patchy timber where it is not well sheltered; fuel beneath standing timber at midslope or higher on a mountain with wind blowing directly at the slope.	All Fuel Models	0.3
FULLY SHELTERED FUELS: Fuel sheltered beneath standing timber on flat or gentle slope or near base of mountain with steep slopes.	All Fuel Models	Open Stands 0.2 Dense Stands 0.1
[1]Fuels usually partially sheltered. [2]Fuels usually fully sheltered.		

28

USDA Forest Service Gen. Tech. Rep. RMRS-GTR-266. 2012

Table 1—Weighting factors for calculating weighted-average dead fuel moisture content, presence of live fuel component, and wind adjustment factor (WAF) for the original 13 and new 40 fire behavior fuel models. Weighting factors assume all herbaceous load is in the 1-h class (full curing). WAF values were estimated using Albini and Baughman's (1979) model of wind reduction over exposed fuelbeds on flat terrain assuming flame height is twice fuelbed depth. Values in this table match those used in BehavePlus, FARSITE, and FlamMap.

Fuel model	Weighting factors 1-h	10-h	100-h	Live fuel Herb	Woody	WAF
1	1.00	0.00	0.00			0.36
2	0.98	0.02	0.00	√		0.36
3	1.00	0.00	0.00			0.44
4	0.95	0.04	0.01		√	0.55
5	0.97	0.03	0.00		√	0.42
6	0.89	0.09	0.02			0.44
7	0.89	0.09	0.02		√	0.44
8	0.94	0.03	0.02			0.28
9	0.99	0.01	0.00			0.28
10	0.94	0.03	0.02		√	0.36
11	0.77	0.17	0.06			0.36
12	0.75	0.19	0.06			0.43
13	0.76	0.18	0.06			0.46
GR1	1.00	0.00	0.00	√		0.31
GR2	1.00	0.00	0.00	√		0.36
GR3	0.98	0.02	0.00	√		0.42
GR4	1.00	0.00	0.00	√		0.42
GR5	1.00	0.00	0.00	√		0.39
GR6	1.00	0.00	0.00	√		0.39
GR7	1.00	0.00	0.00	√		0.46
GR8	0.99	0.01	0.00	√		0.49
GR9	0.99	0.01	0.00	√		0.52
GS1	1.00	0.00	0.00	√	√	0.35
GS2	0.97	0.03	0.00	√	√	0.39
GS3	0.99	0.01	0.00	√	√	0.41
GS4	1.00	0.00	0.00	√	√	0.42
SH1	0.97	0.03	0.00	√	√	0.36
SH2	0.90	0.09	0.01		√	0.36
SH3	0.69	0.31	0.00		√	0.44
SH4	0.93	0.07	0.00		√	0.46
SH5	0.92	0.08	0.00		√	0.55
SH6	0.93	0.07	0.00		√	0.42
SH7	0.80	0.18	0.02		√	0.55
SH8	0.80	0.19	0.01		√	0.46
SH9	0.96	0.04	0.00	√	√	0.50
TU1	0.84	0.11	0.05	√	√	0.33
TU2	0.89	0.09	0.02		√	0.36
TU3	0.99	0.01	0.00	√	√	0.38
TU4	1.00	0.00	0.00		√	0.32
TU5	0.92	0.07	0.01		√	0.36
TL1	0.85	0.10	0.05			0.28
TL2	0.90	0.08	0.02			0.28
TL3	0.76	0.18	0.06			0.29
TL4	0.78	0.13	0.10			0.31
TL5	0.85	0.10	0.05			0.33
TL6	0.97	0.03	0.01			0.29
TL7	0.60	0.15	0.24			0.31
TL8	0.98	0.01	0.00			0.29
TL9	0.96	0.03	0.01			0.33
SB1	0.82	0.09	0.09			0.36
SB2	0.94	0.05	0.01			0.36
SB3	0.97	0.03	0.01			0.38
SB4	0.95	0.03	0.01			0.45

Figure 28—WAF values for the 53 standard fuel models in Scott (2007).

USDA Forest Service Gen. Tech. Rep. RMRS-GTR-266. 2012

29

Scott (2007) also gives a table of sheltered WAF based on canopy cover (figure 29). Values are based on Albini and Baughman (1979), equation [2], with $CR = 1$. Figure 30 shows a comparison of the table and the calculation. BehavePlus also uses equation [2] to calculate sheltered WAF, but allows variable values for crown ratio. While Scott (2007) used the sheltered model when canopy cover was greater than 5 percent, BehavePlus uses the criteria of crown fill portion greater than 5 percent.

Table 3—Wind adjustment factor (WAF) for surface fuel sheltered by a forest canopy (canopy cover greater than 5 percent), as a function of canopy cover (CC). WAF values were stylized for this table based on output from Albini and Baughman's (1979) model of wind reduction by a forest canopy. See table 1 for WAF values to use for unsheltered fuelbeds.

Canopy cover (percent)	WAF
CC ≤ 5	use table 1
5 < CC ≤ 10	0.30
10 < CC ≤ 15	0.25
15 < CC ≤ 30	0.20
30 < CC ≤ 50	0.15
CC > 50	0.10

Figure 29—Sheltered WAF values based on canopy cover in Scott (2007).

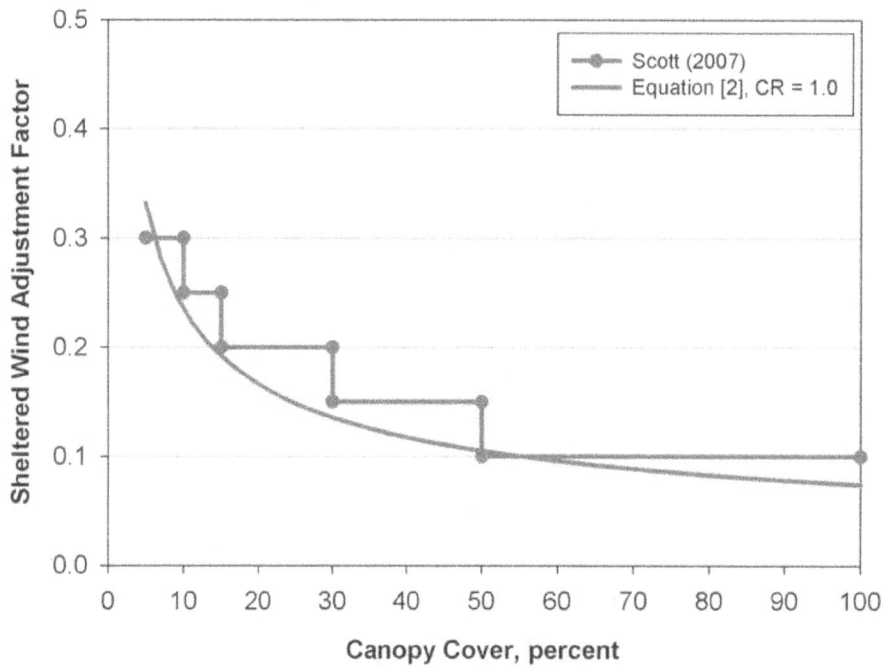

Figure 30—Comparison of sheltered WAF in Scott (2007) table compared to calculation using equation [2] with CR of 1.0.

WAF Calculation Comparison _____

Previous sections addressed WAF values available for use in tabular form. Some fire modeling systems include a calculation of WAF. Table 10 is a summary of methods of calculating WAF in Behave Plus, FARSITE, FlamMap, FSPro, FPA, FuelCalc (Scott, personal communication), Nomographs for the 13 fuel models, the BEHAVE TSTMDL program, and FVS-FFE (Reinhardt and Crookston 2003). The models for sheltered and unsheltered WAF and the criteria of which to use are given in the following sections.

FARSITE Fire Area Simulator

The FARSITE fire area simulator models fire growth under varying conditions of fuel, topography, wind, and fuel moisture. The basic FlamMap function involves independent fire behavior calculations for each point on the landscape under set environmental conditions. The modeling in FARSITE and FlamMap is used in other systems, including FSPro and FPA. All use the method of calculating WAF described by Finney (1998).

FARSITE and FlamMap calculate WAF for each pixel based on the fuel and vegetation values assigned to that pixel. While gridded wind data can account for the effect of terrain on 20-ft wind speed and direction, the adjustment to midflame wind speed does not consider the degree of sheltering of surface fuel due to penetration of the wind into the canopy based on position on the slope or on surrounding canopy cover.

The BehavePlus method of calculating unsheltered WAF was based on that developed for FARSITE (equation [6]) with the assumption that the flame extension above the fuel bed is equal to the fuel bed depth, or that the flame height is twice that of the fuel bed depth. WAF is based on the average wind speed from the top of the fuel bed to twice the fuel bed height. The wording in the FARSITE publication, however, might be misleading: "For nonforested areas midflame windspeed is reduced to a nominal height equal to twice the fuel bed depth." FARSITE uses the average over the height range, not the wind at the set height. As shown by the example calculations in table 4, there is a noteworthy difference in WAF for the average from the top of the fuel bed to twice that height and WAF for the point at twice the fuel bed depth.

The basic calculation of sheltered WAF in FARSITE is the same as that in BehavePlus (equation [2]) but with $CR = 1$. While there was not an error in the FARSITE program, the publication contained an error (Finney 1998 [revised 2004]: p. 18). The constant 0.3066 should have been 0.555 for the equation in metric units. The printed copy of the revised paper in 2004 contained the same error, but the current online version of the publication is correct.

Table 10—Summary of methods of calculating WAF in various systems.

Source	Unsheltered	Sheltered	Sheltered condition
BehavePlus	eq. [6], $H_F = H$	eq. [2], based on CC, CR, and C	eq. [9] and [10], if F>5%
FARSITE, FlamMap, FSPro, FPA	eq. [6], $H_F = H$	eq. [2], based on CC and CH; CR=1	CC>0
FuelCalc	eq. [6], $H_F = H$	eq. [2], based on CC, CR, and CH	If WAF(sheltered)< WAF(unsheltered)
Nomographs (Albini 1976)	0.5	0.5	N/A
TSTMDL program in the old BEHAVE system	eq. [6], H_F = flame length[a]	N/A	N/A
FVS-FFE	0.5	Interpolated from five points; based on CC	CC>5%

[a]Wind speed 0 mi/h, dead moisture 8 percent, live moisture 100 percent, slope 0 percent

USDA Forest Service Gen. Tech. Rep. RMRS-GTR-266. 2012

31

In FARSITE, crown fill portion (fraction) is

$$f = \frac{CC}{100}\frac{\pi}{12}$$

where

CC = canopy cover, percent

This differs from the calculation in BehavePlus (equations [9] and [10]) in two ways. While both methods assume tree crowns are conical, FARSITE includes an additional factor of $\pi/4$ to account for gaps in a square horizontal packing of circular crowns. This addresses the issue of not being able to achieve 100 percent cover with circles. In addition, FARSITE calculates crown fill fraction based on canopy cover without the influence of crown ratio. FARSITE uses $CR = 1$ and $f = F$.

The significant effect of crown ratio on WAF in BehavePlus was shown in figures 20, 21, and 23. Figure 31 compares the intermediate calculation of crown fill portion (f) as a function of canopy cover for BehavePlus and FARSITE.

The square versus circular base assumption has a minor impact. For crown ratio of one, the difference between BehavePlus and FARSITE crown fill portion (f) is due to the $\pi/4$ factor. The resulting WAF in FARSITE is 1.13 times greater than that in BehavePlus, based on a different crown fill portion (f) in equation [12].

FARSITE uses the sheltered WAF model whenever crown cover is greater than zero. For a very low CC of 1 percent, WAF is 0.74 (see figure 11), a value much higher than the WAF that would be calculated for unsheltered fuel. (Sheltered WAF should not be higher than unsheltered WAF.) Although it might seem rare that an area would be categorized with a canopy cover of 1 percent, FARSITE users often change zero canopy cover to a very low value to enable spotting, possibly not realizing that the change also affects WAF and calculated surface fire behavior.

While BehavePlus and FARSITE use the same basic WAF equations, the following is a summary of the differences in implementation:

- BehavePlus uses CC, CH, and CR to find the crown fill portion used in the sheltered WAF calculation. FARSITE uses the same equation with $CR = 1$.
- FARSITE uses the unsheltered WAF model only if canopy cover is zero. BehavePlus uses the unsheltered WAF model if crown fill portion is less than 5 percent.
- FARSITE includes a $\pi/4$ factor that is not in BehavePlus to account for gaps in a square horizontal packing of circular crowns.

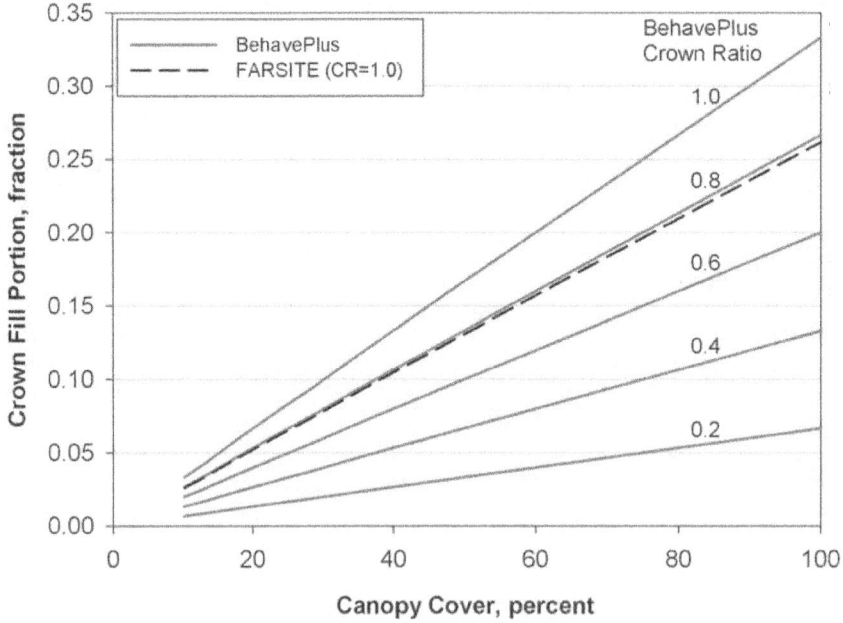

Figure 31—BehavePlus uses CR in the calculation of crown fill portion and, thus, of WAF. FARSITE always uses CR = 1.0 and includes an additional factor of π/4 to account for gaps in a square horizontal packing of circular crowns.

FuelCalc

FuelCalc is a software package that calculates initial fuel quantities, simulates a variety of fuel treatment scenarios, and then calculates potential fire behavior. Wind speed is entered at the 20-ft height. WAF is calculated based on surface fuel and overstory using the same basic Albini and Baughman (1979) models as implemented in BehavePlus. The difference is in the determination of whether to use the sheltered or unsheltered WAF model.

In order to avoid the step change in calculated WAF that occurs in BehavePlus with the change from the sheltered to the unsheltered model (see figure 20), FuelCalc calculates both sheltered and unsheltered and uses the minimum WAF value. The difference occurs for stands with less than 5 percent crown fill portion that are categorized as unsheltered in BehavePlus but might be modeled as sheltered in FuelCalc. Recall that the sheltered model is based on the assumption that wind is constant with height under the top of the canopy.

Figure 32 shows WAF values calculated by FuelCalc for canopy height of 100 ft; crown ratio of 0.1, 0.5, and 0.9; and canopy cover from 0 to 100 percent. The dotted portion of the curves shows where results are different in BehavePlus. For this example, for $CR = 0.1$, BehavePlus would produce WAF = 0.39, the unsheltered value, even for canopy cover of 100 percent, which has a crown fill portion of 2.6 percent. FuelCalc assigns WAF = 0.23 — the minimum of the sheltered value 0.39 and the unsheltered value 0.23.

Table 11 shows selected values from the plot with a comparison of BehavePlus and FuelCalc WAF values and associated flame length. When there is a difference, FuelCalc produces lower modeled fire behavior due to the sheltered assumption and the lower WAF (greater reduction).

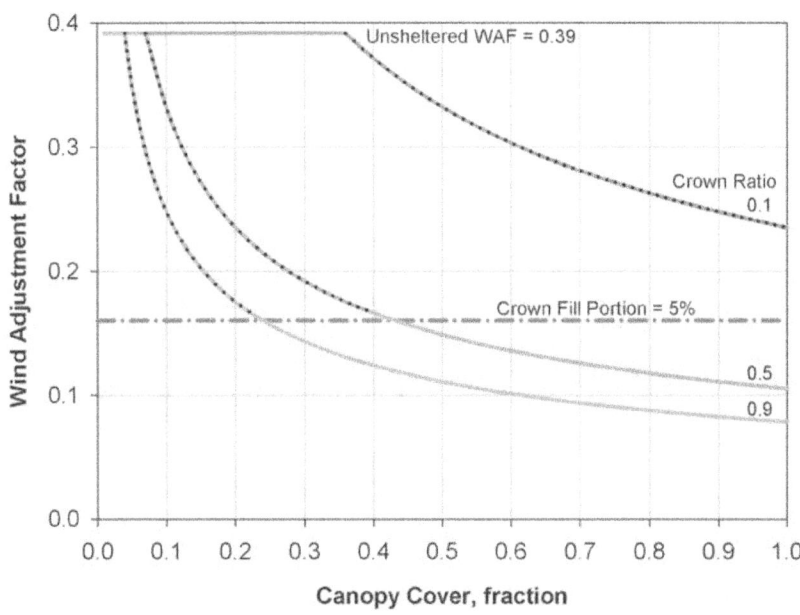

Figure 32—WAF values calculated by FuelCalc. Canopy height is 100 ft. There are differences from BehavePlus (dotted portion of the curves) when crown fill portion is less than 5 percent and the sheltered WAF is less than the unsheltered WAF value.

Table 11—Comparison of FuelCalc and BehavePlus WAF values and associated flame length. When there is a difference (bold), FuelCalc results are lower.

Canopy cover, percent	FuelCalc			BehavePlus		
	WAF[a]	Midflame wind, mi/h	Flame Length[b], ft	WAF	Midflame wind, mi/h	Flame Length[b], ft
5	0.39	7.8	12.1	0.39	7.8	12.1
10	**0.33**	**6.6**	**10.9**	**0.39**	**7.8**	**12.1**
20	**0.23**	**4.6**	**8.8**	**0.39**	**7.8**	**12.1**
30	**0.19**	**3.8**	**7.8**	**0.39**	**7.8**	**12.1**
40	**0.17**	**3.4**	**7.3**	**0.39**	**7.8**	**12.1**
50	0.15	3.0	6.8	0.15	3.0	6.8
60	0.14	2.8	6.6	0.14	2.8	6.6

[a] Canopy height 100 ft, crown ratio 0.5
[b] Fuel model GR5 (low load, humid climate grass), dead moisture 5 percent, live moisture 75 percent, 20-ft wind 20 mi/h, slope 0 percent.

USDA Forest Service Gen. Tech. Rep. RMRS-GTR-266. 2012

33

BEHAVE

The BEHAVE fire behavior prediction and fuel modeling system was the predecessor to the BehavePlus fire modeling system. WAF was not calculated in the fire behavior prediction portion of BEHAVE (Andrews 1986; Andrews and Chase 1989). The fuel modeling program TSTMDL calculated an unsheltered WAF for custom fuel models (Burgan and Rothermel 1984). WAF was calculated as described in (Rothermel 1983). If a standard fuel model was saved as a custom fuel model, the reported WAF could be different due to the adjustments that Rothermel made to the calculated values to produce his table. The method of calculating WAF in the TST-MDL program of BEHAVE is different from that used in BehavePlus.

FVS-FFE

The fire and fuels extension to the forest vegetation simulator (FVS-FFE) simulates fuel dynamics and potential fire behavior over time, in the context of stand development and management. It is used to better understand and display the consequences of alternative management actions. Wind is not a critical component of the modeling, given that a default value of 20 mi/h can be used for 20-ft wind speed. The 20-ft wind speed is converted to midflame wind speed by multiplying it by what the authors call "a correction factor" based on the canopy cover in the stand (figure 33). For canopy cover from 0 to 5 percent, WAF is 0.5. Unsheltered WAF is therefore constant and does not depend on fuel model or surface fuel bed depth. A comparison of the FVS-FFE values to equation [2], with $CR = 1$ is shown in figure 34.

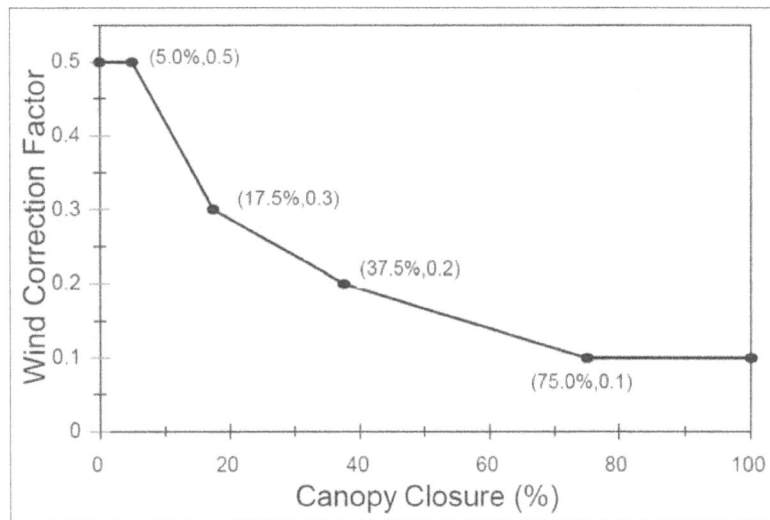

Figure 33—WAF values used in FVS-FFE are a function of CC. Results are interpolated between the six points as labeled on the plot. From Reinhardt and Crookston (2003). The authors used the term "Wind Correction Factor" for "Wind Adjustment Factor" and "Canopy Closure" for "Canopy Cover."

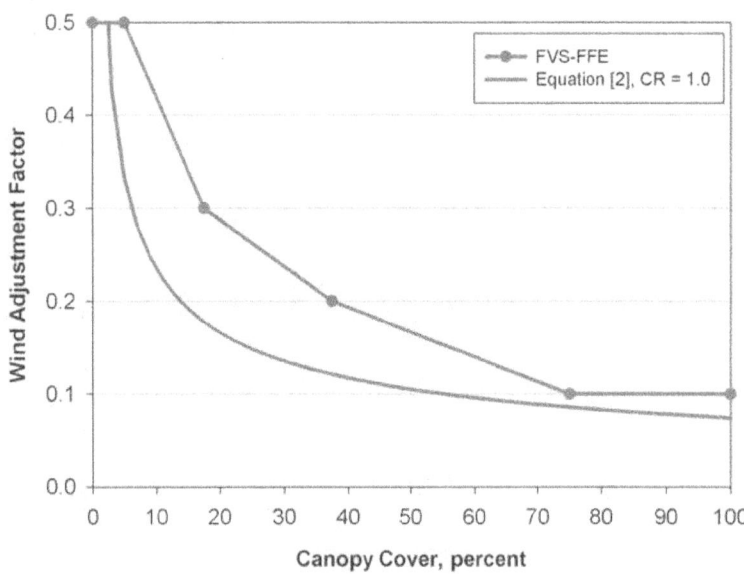

Figure 34—WAF values used in FVS-FFE compared to calculated values according to equation [2] with CR = 1.

WAF for NFDRS

To this point, we have discussed fire behavior modeling applications, which produce specific fire behavior values such as rate of spread and flame length. NFDRS, on the other hand, produces indices to indicate seasonal fire potential. Fire weather stations are located in the open, with no trees and no deep surface fuel. NFDRS is based on a worst-case assumption, so it doesn't specifically consider sheltered conditions. The basis of the NFDRS calculations is the Rothermel fire spread model, which requires wind at the midflame height. Wind is measured and forecast for NFDRS at 20 ft above the ground.

The 1972 NFDRS (Deeming and others 1972) was replaced by a major update in 1978 (Deeming and others 1977). A 1988 update offered additional options to the 1978 system (Burgan 1988). The current system allows users to select either 1978 fuel models or 1988 fuel models. The WAF values for the 1978 and 1988 NFDRS and the retired National Fire Management Analysis System (NFMAS) (USDA Forest Service 1983), which used NFDRS fuel models, are given in table 12.

The 1972 NFDRS used WAF (which was called r) of 0.5 for the nine fuel models. Schroeder and others (1972: p. 83-92) selected that value after in-depth analysis similar to that of Albini and Baughman (1979): "The ratio of the 6 meter windspeed to the mid-flame height windspeed gave values of r between 0.4 and 0.6 for all the fuel models over the range of windspeeds considered in the National Fire-Danger Rating System. Because of the general nature of the fuel models, the variability of r, we have chosen to set r equal to 0.5 until such time as fuel descriptions and meteorological instrumentation permit these fine distinctions to be properly utilized."

The 1978 NFDRS assigned a WAF to each of the 20 fuel models (Cohen and Deeming 1985). (The table of 1978 fuel model descriptions in Burgan [1988] incorrectly listed the WAF for fuel model E as 0.5.) These WAF values were assigned prior to Albini and Baughman (1979) publishing the modeling basis for WAF calculations used for fire behavior prediction. The grouping for NFDRS was described as WAF = 0.6 for grass models, 0.5 for shrub and brush models, and 0.4 for timber models (Bradshaw and others 1983).

The 1988 NFDRS optional update uses a constant WAF if the fuel model has no live woody component or if the live woody vegetation is designated as evergreen. While not listed in Burgan (1988), the 88 NFDRS constant WAF values in table 12 were taken from the computer code. There is a change from the 78 NFDRS values for fuel models L, N, P, Q, and U. A variable WAF is used

Table 12—WAF values assigned to each of the NFDRS for the 1978 and 1988 system and for the now retired NFMAS system.

	Fuel Model	78 NFDRS	88 NFDRS	88 NFDRS Min – Max[a]	NFMAS
A	Western grasses (annual)	0.6	0.6		0.36
B	California chaparral	0.5	0.5	0.5 – 0.5	0.55
C	Pine-grass savanna	0.4	0.4	0.3 – 0.5	0.25
D	Southern rough	0.4	0.4	0.4 – 0.4	0.12
E	Hardwood litter (winter)	0.4	0.4	0.3 – 0.5	0.25
F	Intermediate brush	0.5	0.5	0.5 – 0.5	0.42
G	Short needle (heavy dead)	0.4	0.4	0.3 – 0.3	0.12
H	Short needle (normal dead)	0.4	0.4	0.3 – 0.3	0.17
I	Heavy slash	0.5	0.5		0.46
J	Intermediate slash	0.5	0.5		0.43
K	Light slash	0.5	0.5		0.36
L	Western grasses (perennial)	0.6	0.5		0.44
N	Sawgrass	0.6	0.5	0.5 – 0.5	0.55
O	High pocosin	0.5	0.5	0.5 – 0.5	0.55
P	Southern pine plantation	0.4	0.3	0.3 – 0.3	0.12
Q	Alaska black spruce	0.4	0.2	0.2 – 0.3	0.63
R	Hardwood litter (summer)	0.4	0.4	0.3 – 0.5	0.08
S	Tundra	0.6	0.6	0.6 – 0.6	0.45
T	Sagebrush-grass	0.6	0.6	0.6 – 0.6	0.42
U	Western pines	0.4	0.3	0.3 – 0.3	0.12

[a]Used to calculate WAF that changes with season when live woody fuel is designated as deciduous.
Blank cells indicate fuel models without live woody fuel.

USDA Forest Service Gen. Tech. Rep. RMRS-GTR-266. 2012

35

for fuel types for which live woody fuel is designated as deciduous. WAF is set to its maximum value during the winter. (Higher WAF causes less wind reduction due to leaf drop and higher wind speeds.) WAF decreases during the spring and increases during the fall as a function of the woody greenness factor. WAF is set to its minimum value during the summer when shrubs are fully green. (Lower WAF causes more wind reduction and lower wind speeds.) Note in table 12 that the maximum is equal to minimum WAF for some fuel models, so the variable WAF is applied only to fuel models C, E, Q, and R. Note also that designating live woody fuel as deciduous for 1988 fuel models G and H effectively changes the WAF from 0.4 to 0.3.

In addition, for all 1988 fuel models, if more than 0.1 inch of precipitation occurred either on the current or the previous day, the WAF is multiplied by 0.3. "This correction reduces the sensitivity of the 1988 NFDRS to wind until the dead fuels have had at least 1 day of drying" (Burgan 1988). This is merely an artificial way to influence index values and is not based on any actual effect on the wind.

NFMAS was a fire planning system that used fire danger fuel models. Calculations were aimed at estimating fire behavior for the planning application rather than to produce fire danger indices as in NFDRS. The NFMAS WAF values in table 12 are given here for historical documentation. NFMAS has been retired and replaced by FPA, which uses fire behavior fuel models and the modeling in FlamMap.

Discussion

Of the many aspects of wind that affect fire behavior, WAF addresses only one. It reduces the wind speed at 20 ft above the vegetation to a value at midflame height as needed by Rothermel's surface fire spread model. Other means are used to determine variation in 20-ft wind speed and direction across the landscape, as well as temporal changes from gusts to front passages.

Decisions that are supported by fire modeling can be influenced by the WAF. It is important that a user be aware of the technical foundation of the models with all of the associated assumptions and limitations.

Model Limitations

As is the case with all models, WAF models are based on simplifying assumptions. Following is from the section "Applicability of Results" in Albini and Baughman (1979):

The numerical results derived in this report are subject to the restrictions listed below. The reader is cautioned to be certain that the specified conditions prevail when using these results.

1. Flat terrain has been assumed throughout. If the terrain has substantial slope or roughness, the windfield will reflect this fact, and substantial deviations from these results may occur.

2. Adequate fetch to establish a uniform friction layer has been assumed. The definition of "adequate" fetch is the subject of current research (Shaw 1977), so numerical limits cannot be stated at this time. But near forest edges, lakeshores, or transitions in surface vegetation cover, the results given here may not be accurate.

3. A "well-behaved" windfield is modeled by the relationships herein. If the windfield is not steady, but fluctuates significantly in speed, direction, or both, the friction layer will be continually in a transient state as it responds to the forces at play. During the periods of such variability the results given here may not be applicable.

4. Any interaction between the fire and the windfield that substantially influences the speed or direction of the wind should invalidate these results. We have dealt here with a windfield whose structure is dominated by the influence of the vegetation cover on the friction layer and any factor that disturbs this condition negates the validity of the results given here.

An additional limitation is the assumption of a neutral stable atmosphere near the ground. And convective slope winds have a different velocity profile than that shown in figure 1. Rothermel (1983) noted that "the type of wind driving the fire is very important and must be known to make proper interpretation of midflame windspeed."

The model for WAF, based on average wind speed over a height range, is consistent with the wind tunnel data used in developing the spread model. Alternate definitions of midflame height at a specific height, using the same wind profile, give significantly different WAF results (see table 4). There will always be differences between the model results and a wind measurement taken at eye level because the observation is not an average over a height range.

It is well known that many influencing factors are not considered in the simple Albini and Baughman models. For example, Schroeder and Buck (1970) described the effects of vegetation on wind in their comprehensive "Fire Weather" publication. Among the influences they describe: "In forest stands that are open beneath the main

36

USDA Forest Service Gen. Tech. Rep. RMRS-GTR-266. 2012

tree canopy, air speed increases with height above the surface to the middle of the trunk space, and then decreases again in the canopy zone." The WAF model is based on the assumption that wind is constant under the canopy.

Limitations of the WAF models should be considered in conjunction with limitations of all associated models and with ability to describe the required input values. Overstory trees, for example, are not uniformly shaped cones. The same canopy cover can result from many narrow trees or fewer broad ones. The surface fire spread model is based on the assumption that the surface fuels are uniform and continuous. Geospatial fire modeling systems use data for which conditions are assumed constant for each pixel (possibly 30 m across). It is the responsibility of a model user to be aware of all of the many limitations in appropriate application of model results.

Model limitations should also be considered in the context of application. Limitations of individual models (such as WAF) might be minor in the context of a fire growth simulation that involves thousands of calculations and variables. On the other hand, the limitation of the modeling to determine the point at which fuels are sheltered from the wind by overstory can be significant in fuel treatment assessments. BehavePlus is designed to encourage users to generate tables and graphs to examine the effect of input selections on results rather than merely supplying values for each input variable and getting a result from a single calculation.

Modeling Applications

When Albini and Baughman developed WAF models, fire behavior analysts predicted wildfire behavior using tables, graphs, and nomographs (Albini 1976b; Rothermel 1983). There was an appropriate reliance on experience and judgment in determining sheltering of fuels from the wind to select a WAF value. That application continues. A user of nomographs, BehavePlus, or other similar systems can and should use judgment to determine WAF based not only on conditions at a point, but on wind direction, nearby vegetation, location on the slope, and the ability of wind to penetrate the overstory.

While judgment is an important component of predicting wildfire behavior, fire planning applications, including fuel hazard assessment, may be better served by the consistency and repeatability of models. Calculation of WAF can have a large impact on results, especially when conditions are close to the point of transition between sheltered and unsheltered fuel. In addition there is the limitation of using the canopy description only at the fuel treatment site to calculate WAF. Two stands with the same overstory and understory and the same 20-ft wind speed in reality could have different potential fire behavior due to the influence of surrounding vegetation on the wind. The midflame wind speed in a small, thinned area surrounded by closed timber would differ from that in a large, thinned area adjacent to a meadow. A modeler should find the appropriate balance between calculations and judgment.

The use of fire models for wildland fire management has greatly expanded since the 1970s. Computer systems are ever more complex and sophisticated. A fire growth simulation system such as FARSITE necessarily relies on a calculated WAF. Judgment has no place in determining WAF for thousands of pixels. The original FARSITE used a wind field that changed in time but was constant over the landscape. As noted by Finney (1998) in describing his implementation of WAF calculations, "Variation would undoubtedly occur with stands of mixed species, multiple strata, different crown shapes, and tree arrangement. However, given the burden of additional input requirements, further refinement could not be justified without models of spatially dynamic wind fields that reflect the influence of topography, vegetation roughness, and neighboring vegetation structure."

Models that adjust the 20-ft wind across the terrain are now available at the scale needed by FARSITE and other geospatial fire modeling systems (Wind Ninja and Wind Wizard) (Butler and others 2006; Forthofer and others 2009). FARSITE then adjusts the spatially variable 20-ft wind speed to midflame height based on vegetation for each pixel and not adjacent pixels, wind direction, or terrain. The question of the burden of additional input requirements remains.

Model Needs

This report first described implementation of WAF models in BehavePlus followed by WAF in other applications, with emphasis on the differences. Even though most applications cite Albini and Baughman (1979), there are differences in the implementation and in the results. The question about the need for consistency among fire modeling systems should be asked in conjunction with an assessment of the impact of change. It may seem logical for all applications to use the same approach. But while an internal, transparent, change to equations might be easy for a programmer, a change in calculated results can be unsettling. The impact of redoing analyses, plans, and reports that used model results can be significant and perhaps unnecessary. Given differences in WAF modeling approaches and the impact on results,

USDA Forest Service Gen. Tech. Rep. RMRS-GTR-266. 2012

37

fire modeling results should be reported along with the source (reference, computer program, version number, etc.), and possibly model assumptions.

A good solution would be a new and improved WAF model that is well documented and can uniformly be implemented in a range of applications that require mid-flame wind speed. Such an improvement could overcome some of the current limitations such as the transition between models for unsheltered and sheltered fuels and consideration of adequate fetch and terrain on penetration of the wind through the overstory.

While wind profile modeling is useful to all fire behavior models, current WAF modeling is aimed at the requirements of the Rothermel surface fire spread model. Future fire models might be able to utilize or even require wind speed and direction that vary in time and space.

A modeling effort inherently requires assumptions on what is relevant to the effort. Uncertainties in fuel characterization, fuel moisture variation, and complex wind behavior should be considered. There is a large range in fire modeling approaches and products. At one extreme are CFD (computational fluid dynamics) models that model specifics of air flow through the canopy, if there are fuel and vegetation data to feed the model. At the other extreme are non-computer based guides for use on the fireline. The need continues for general guidelines that incorporate influencing factors for fire behavior and safety.

Albini and Baughman's WAF modeling has served us well. Their models are included in applications that go well beyond the initial tables designed to be used by an experienced fire behavior analyst who can make adjustments based on judgment. Albini and Baughman (1979) stated that "… this effort is seen as a small first step in the direction of a more complete description of the complex phenomena with which we are dealing."

References _____

Albini, Frank A. 1976a. Computer-based models of wildland fire behavior: a user's manual. Ogden, UT: U.S. Department of Agriculture, Forest Service, Intermountain Forest and Range Experiment Station. 68 p.

Albini, Frank A. 1976b. Estimating wildfire behavior and effects. Gen. Tech. Rep. INT-30. Ogden, UT: U.S. Department of Agriculture, Forest Service, Intermountain Forest and Range Experiment Station. 92 p.

Albini, Frank A.; Baughman, Robert G. 1979. Estimating windspeeds for predicting wildland fire behavior. Res. Pap. INT-221. Ogden, UT: U.S. Department of Agriculture, Forest Service, Intermountain Forest and Range Experiment Station. 12 p.

Anderson, Hal E. 1982. Aids to determining fuel models for estimating fire behavior. Gen. Tech. Rep. INT-122. Ogden, UT: U.S. Department of Agriculture, Forest Service, Intermountain Forest and Range Experiment Station. 22 p.

Andrews, Patricia L. 1986. BEHAVE: fire behavior prediction and fuel modeling system–BURN subsystem, part 1. Gen. Tech. Rep. INT-194. Ogden, UT: U.S. Department of Agriculture, Forest Service, Intermountain Research Station. 130 p.

Andrews, Patricia L. 2007. BehavePlus fire modeling system: past, present, and future. In: Proceedings of 7th Symposium on Fire and Forest Meteorology; 2007 October 23-25; Bar Harbor, ME. Boston, MA: American Meteorological Society. 13 p.

Andrews, Patricia L. 2009. BehavePlus fire modeling system, version 5.0: Variables. Gen. Tech. Rep. RMRS-GTR-213WWW Revised. Fort Collins, CO: Department of Agriculture, Forest Service, Rocky Mountain Research Station. 111 p.

Andrews, Patricia L. 2011. Do you BEHAVE? Application of the BehavePlus fire modeling system. In: Proceedings of 3rd Fire Behavior and Fuels Conference; 2010 October 25-29; Spokane, WA. Missoula, MT: International Association of Wildland Fire. 17 p.

Andrews, Patricia L.; Chase, Carolyn. H. 1989. BEHAVE: fire behavior prediction and fuel modeling system–BURN subsystem, part 2. Gen. Tech. Rep. INT-260. Ogden, UT: U.S. Department of Agriculture, Forest Service, Intermountain Research Station. 93 p.

Baughman, Robert G.; Albini, Frank A. 1980. Estimating midflame windspeeds. In: Proceedings of Sixth Conference on Fire and Forest Meteorology; 1980 April 22-24; Seattle, WA. Washington, DC: Society of American Foresters: 88-92.

Bradshaw, Larry S.; Deeming, John E.; Burgan, Robert E.; Cohen, Jack D. 1983. The 1978 National Fire-Danger Rating System: technical documentation. Gen. Tech. Rep. INT-169. Ogden, UT: U.S. Department of Agriculture, Forest Service, Intermountain Forest and Range Experiment Station. 44 p.

Bradshaw, Larry S.; Petrescu, Gene.; Grenfell, Isaac. 2003. An initial analysis of relationships between 2- and 10-minute averaged winds at 10, 6, and 1.8 meters: implications for fire behavior and danger applications. In: 2nd International Wildland Fire Ecology and Fire Management Congress and 5th Symposium on Fire and Forest Meteorology; 2003 November 16-20; Orlando, FL. Boston, MA: American Meteorological Society. 5 p.

Burgan, Robert E. 1988. 1988 revisions to the 1978 National Fire-Danger Rating System. Res. Pap. SE-273. Asheville, NC: U.S. Department of Agriculture, Forest Service, Southeastern Forest Experiment Station. 39 p.

Burgan, Robert E.; Rothermel, Richard C. 1984. BEHAVE: fire behavior prediction and fuel modeling system–FUEL subsystem. Gen. Tech. Rep. INT-167. Ogden, UT: U.S. Department of Agriculture, Forest Service, Intermountain Forest and Range Experiment Station. 126 p.

Butler, Bret W.; Finney, Mark; Bradshaw, Larry; Forthofer, Jason; McHugh, Chuck; Stratton, Rick; Jimenez, Dan. 2006. WindWizard: a new tool for fire management decision support. In: Andrews, P. L.; Butler, B. W., comps. Fuels management—How to measure success: conference proceedings; 2006 March 28-30; Portland, OR. Proc. RMRS-P-41. Fort Collins, CO: U.S. Department of Agriculture, Forest Service, Rocky Mountain Research Station: 787-796.

Cohen, Jack D.; Deeming, John E. 1985. The National Fire-Danger Rating System: basic equations. Gen. Tech. Rep. PSW-82. Berkeley, CA: U.S. Department of Agriculture, Forest Service, Pacific Southwest Forest and Range Experiment Station. 16 p.

Deeming, John E.; Burgan, Robert E.; Cohen, Jack D. 1977. The National Fire-Danger Rating System–1978. Gen. Tech. Rep. INT-39. Ogden, UT: U.S. Department of Agriculture, Forest Service, Intermountain Forest and Range Experiment Station. 63 p.

Deeming, John E.; Lancaster, James W.; Fosberg, Michael A.; Furman, R. William; Schroeder, Mark J. 1972. National Fire-Danger Rating System. Res. Pap. RM-84. Fort Collins, CO: U.S. Department of Agriculture, Forest Service, Rocky Mountain Forest and Range Experiment Station. 165 p.

Finney, Mark A. 1998 [revised 2004]. FARSITE: Fire Area Simulator—model development and evaluation. Res. Pap. RMRS-RP-4. Ogden, UT: U.S. Department of Agriculture, Forest Service, Rocky Mountain Research Station. 47 p. Corrected version available: http://www.fs.fed.us/rm/pubs/rmrs_rp004.pdf [September 29, 2011].

Finney, Mark A. 2006. An overview of FlamMap fire modeling capabilities. In: Andrews, P. L.; Butler, B. W., comps. Fuels management—How to measure success: conference proceedings; 2006 March 28-30; Portland, OR. Proc. RMRS-P-41. Fort Collins, CO: U.S. Department of Agriculture, Forest Service, Rocky Mountain Research Station: 213-220.

Finney, Mark A.; Grenfell, Isaac C.; McHugh, Charles W.; Seli, Robert C.; Trethewey, Diane; Stratton, Richard D.; Brittain, Stuart. 2010. A method for ensemble wildland fire simulation. Environmental Modeling and Assessment. 16(2): 153-167.

Finney, Mark A.; McHugh, Charles W.; Grenfell, Isaac C.; Riley, Karin L.; Short, Karen C. 2011. A simulation of probabilistic wildfire risk components for the continental United States. Stochastic Environmental Research and Risk Assessment. 25(7): 973-1000.

Fischer, William C.; Hardy, Charles E. 1972. Fire-weather observer's handbook. Agric. Handb. 494. Ogden, UT: U.S. Department of Agriculture, Forest Service, Intermountain Forest and Range Experiment Station. 152 p.

Forthofer, Jason; Shannon, Kyle; Butler, Bret. 2009. Simulating diurnally driven slope winds with WindNinja. In: Proceedings of the 8th Symposium on Fire and Forest Meteorology; 2009 October 13-15; Kalispell, MT. Boston, MA: American Meteorological Society. 10 p.

Heinsch, Faith Ann; Andrews, Patricia L. 2010. BehavePlus fire modeling system, version 5.0: Design and Features. Gen. Tech. Rep. RMRS-GTR-249. Fort Collins, CO: U.S. Department of Agriculture, Forest Service, Rocky Mountain Research Station. 111 p.

Jennings, Stephen B.; Brown, Nick D.; Sheil, Douglas. 1999. Assessing forest canopies and understorey illumination: canopy closure, canopy cover and other measures. Forestry. 72(1): 59-73.

McArthur, Alan G. 1969. The Tasmanian bushfires of 7th February, 1967, and associated fire behavior characteristics. In: Mass fire symposium: the technical cooperation programme, Panel N2 working group. Forest Research Institute, Canberra, Australia. 23 p.

McPherson, Renee A.; Fiebrich, Christopher A.; Crawford, Kenneth C.; [and others]. 2007. Statewide monitoring of the mesoscale environment: a technical update on the Oklahoma Mesonet. Journal of Atmospheric and Oceanic Technology. 24(3): 301-321.

National Wildfire Coordinating Group [NWCG]. 2006. NWCG fireline handbook appendix B: fire behavior. PMS 410-2/NFES 2165. Boise, ID: National Interagency Fire Center. 124 p.

Norum, Rodney A. 1983. Wind adjustment factors for predicting fire behavior in three fuel types in Alsaka. Res. Pap. PNW-309. Portland, OR: U.S. Department of Agriculture, Forest Service, Pacific Northwest Forest and Range Experiment Station. 5 p.

Ottmar, Roger D.; Sandberg, David V.; Riccardi, Cynthia L.; Prichard, Susan J. 2007. An overview of the Fuel Characteristic Classification System–quantifying, classifying, and creating fuelbeds for resource planning. Canadian Journal of Forest Research. 37(12): 2383-2393.

Reinhardt, Elizabeth D.; Crookston, Nicholas L. 2003. The Fire and Fuels Extension to the Forest Vegetation Simulator. Gen. Tech. Rep. RMRS-GTR-116. Ogden, UT: U.S. Department of Agriculture, Forest Service, Rocky Mountain Research Station. 209 p.

Reinhardt, Elizabeth D.; Keane, Robert E.; Brown, James K. 1997. First Order Fire Effects Model: FOFEM 4.0, user's guide. Gen. Tech. Rep. INT-GTR-344. Ogden, UT: U.S. Department of Agriculture, Forest Service, Intermountain Research Station. 65 p.

Rothermel, Richard C. 1965. Low airspeed differential pressure integrating system. Res. Note INT-37. Ogden, UT: U.S. Department of Agriculture, Forest Service, Intermountain Forest and Range Experiment Station. 8 p.

Rothermel, Richard C. 1967. Airflow characteristics–wind tunnels and combustion facilities–Northern Forest Fire Laboratory. Missoula, MT: U.S. Department of Agriculture, Forest Service, Intermountain Forest and Range Experiment Station. 32 p.

Rothermel, Richard C. 1972. A mathematical model for predicting fire spread in wildland fuels. Res. Pap. INT-115. Ogden, UT: U.S. Department of Agriculture, Forest Service, Intermountain Forest and Range Experiment Station. 40 p.

Rothermel, Richard C. 1983. How to predict the spread and intensity of forest and range fires. Gen. Tech. Rep. INT-143. Ogden, UT: U.S. Department of Agriculture, Forest Service, Intermountain Forest and Range Experiment Station. 161 p.

Rothermel, Richard C.; Anderson, Hal E. 1966. Fire spread characteristics determined in the laboratory. Res. Pap. INT-30. Ogden, UT: U.S. Department of Agriculture, Forest Service, Intermountain Forest and Range Experiment Station. 34 p.

Schroeder, Mark J.; Buck, Charles C. 1970. Fire weather...A guide to application of meteorological information to forest fire control operations. Agric. Handb. 360. Washington, DC: U.S. Department of Agriculture, Forest Service. 229 p.

Schroeder, Mark J.; Fosberg, Michael A.; Lancaster, James W.; Deeming, John E.; Furman, R. William. 1972. Technical development of the National Fire-Danger Rating System. Review Draft. Unpublished paper on file at: U.S. Department of Agriculture, Forest Service, Rocky Mountain Research Station, Fire Sciences Laboratory, Missoula, MT. 151 p.

Scott, Joe H. 1998. NEXUS: a system for assessing crown fire hazard. Fire Management Notes 59(2): 20-24.

Scott, Joe H. 2007. Nomographs for estimating surface fire behavior characteristics. Gen. Tech. Rep. RMRS-GTR-192. Fort Collins, CO: U.S. Department of Agriculture, Forest Service, Rocky Mountain Research Station. 119 p.

Scott, Joe H. 2010. [Email to Patricia L. Andrews]. July 20. FuelCalc 1.0 Reference Guide, Draft. On file at: U.S. Department of Agriculture, Forest Service, Rocky Mountain Research Station, Fire Sciences Laboratory, Missoula, MT; Fire, Fuel, and Smoke Science Program files.

Scott, Joe H.; Burgan, Robert E. 2005. Standard fire behavior fuel models: a comprehensive set for use with Rothermel's surface fire spread model. Gen. Tech. Rep. RMRS-GTR-153. Fort Collins, CO: U.S. Department of Agriculture, Forest Service, Rocky Mountain Research Station. 72 p.

Shaw, Roger H. 1977. Secondary wind speed maxima inside plant canopies. Journal of Applied Meteorology. 16(5): 514-521.

Sutton, O. Graham. 1953. Micrometeorology. New York: McGraw-Hill. 333 p.

Turner, Jack A.; Lawson, Bruce D. 1978. Weather in the Canadian Forest Fire Danger Rating System: a user's guide to national standards and practices. Information Report BC-X-177. Victoria, British Columbia, Canada: Environment Canada, Canadian Forest Service, Pacific Forest Research Centre.

U.S. Department of Agriculture [USDA], Forest Service. 1983. Fire management analysis and planning handbook. For. Serv. Handb. 5109-19. Washington, DC: U.S. Department of Agriculture, Forest Service. 100 p.

U.S. Department of Agriculture [USDA]; U.S. Department of the Interior [USDI]. 2001. Developing an interagency, landscape-scale fire planning analysis and budget tool, Report to the National Fire Plan Coordinators.

USDA Forest Service Gen. Tech. Rep. RMRS-GTR-266. 2012

39

www.ingramcontent.com/pod-product-compliance
Lightning Source LLC
Chambersburg PA
CBHW082159290526
45794CB00008B/3361